ΕΥΡΙΠΙΔΟΥ EURIPIDES'

Βάκχαι *Bacchae*

A Dual Language Edition

Greek Text Edited by
Gilbert Murray

English Translation and Notes by
Ian Johnston

Edited by
Evan Hayes and Stephen Nimis

FAENUM PUBLISHING
OXFORD, OHIO

Euripides Bacchae: *A Dual Language Edition*
First Edition

© 2015 by Faenum Publishing

ISBN-10: 1940997135
ISBN-13: 9781940997131

Published by Faenum Publishing, Ltd.
Cover Design: Evan Hayes

for Geoffrey (1974-1997)

οἵη περ φύλλων γενεὴ τοίη δὲ καὶ ἀνδρῶν.
φύλλα τὰ μέν τ᾽ ἄνεμος χαμάδις χέει, ἄλλα δέ θ᾽ ὕλη
τηλεθόωσα φύει, ἔαρος δ᾽ ἐπιγίγνεται ὥρη:
ὡς ἀνδρῶν γενεὴ ἣ μὲν φύει ἣ δ᾽ ἀπολήγει.

Generations of men are like the leaves.
In winter, winds blow them down to earth,
but then, when spring season comes again,
the budding wood grows more. And so with men:
one generation grows, another dies away.   (*Iliad* 6)

TABLE OF CONTENTS

EDITORS' NOTE

This volume presents the Ancient Greek text of Euripides' *Bacchae* with a facing English translation. The Greek text is that of Gilbert Murray (1913), from the Oxford Classical Texts series, which is in the public domain and available as a pdf. This text has also been digitized by the Perseus Project (perseus.tufts.edu). The English translation and accompanying notes are those of Ian Johnston of Vancouver Island University, Nanaimo, BC. This translation is available freely online (records.viu.ca/~johnstoi/). We have reset both texts, making a number of very minor corrections and modifications, and placed them on opposing pages. This facing-page format will be useful to those wishing to read the English translation while looking at version of the Greek original, or vice versa.

Note that some discrepancies exists between the Greek text and English translation. There is an important gap of 50 lines or more in Euripides' manuscript between lines 1329 and 1330 of the Greek text. Since the content of the missing lines is fairly well known, this translation has attempted to provide a reconstructed text for the missing portion. Occasionally readings from other editions of or commentaries on Euripides' Greek text are used, accounting for some minor departures from Murray.

An Introductory Note to Euripides' *Bacchae*
by Ian Johnston

Introduction

Euripides' *Bacchae*, the last extant classical Greek tragedy, has for a long time been the focus of an intense interpretative argument, probably more so than any other Greek tragedy (especially in the wide range of very different interpretations the play). In this necessarily brief introduction, I wish to sketch out some details of the source of this disagreement and review some of the more common interpretative possibilities. In the course of this discussion, my own preferences will be clear enough, but I hope to do justice to some viewpoints with which I disagree.

Some Obvious Initial Points

To start with, let me review some of the more obvious and important facts of the play, things about which we are unlikely to disagree and which any interpretation is going to have to take into account. After this quick and brief review of the salient points, I'll address some of the ways people have sought to interpret them.

First, the central dramatic action of the *Bacchae*--the play's most obvious and important feature--is an invasion of Greece by an Asian religion (something which may well have a historical basis from a time well before Euripides, but that is not our concern here). The opening scenes of the play repeatedly stress the non-Greek qualities and origins of the followers of Dionysus, tell us that they have been involved in a sweep through Asia Minor, converting cities as they go, and indicate clearly that Thebes is the first entirely Greek city subject to this new force, the first stop in what is to be a continuing campaign of forceful conversion of Greek city-states. Dionysus may have been born in Thebes (more about that later), but he and his followers identify themselves and their cause repeatedly as an invasion of Greece by Asian (non-Greek) ways--and what he brings with him is also seen by the Greeks (at least by Pentheus) as something non-Greek, something new and threatening (the difference is, of course, emphatically brought out by the clothing and movements of the chorus in contrast to the clothing and movements of the citizens of Thebes).

It's also clear enough what this religion involves, a rapturous group experience featuring dancing, costumes, music, wine, and ecstatic release out in nature away from the city (in the wild, potentially dangerous nature of the mountains, not in the safer cultivated areas). It is presented to us as a primarily (but not exclusively) female experience, one which takes women of all ages away from their homes and their responsibilities in the polis and confers on them amazingly irrational powers, beyond the traditional controls exercised by the male rulers of the city, and brings them into harmony with wild nature (most obviously symbolized by the dancing in bare feet). In the Bacchic celebrations the traditional lines of division between human beings and animals and between different groups of human beings (social and gender differences) break down and disappear or are transformed. The play stresses the beauty, energy, creativity, and communal joy of this Bacchic ritual, while at the same time repeatedly informing us of the destructive potential latent in it.

The central conflict in the play focuses on the clash between this new religion and the traditional Greek way of life--both the customary political authority (embodied in Pentheus) and the long-standing religious and social attitudes (manifested most clearly by Tiresias and Cadmus, two figures of major symbolic importance in traditional Greek literature and myth). These characters are faced with the issue of how they should respond to something very foreign to what they are used to. They discuss the matter, argue amongst themselves, and make different decisions. The play thus forces us to examine a range of options and to confront the question about how one should deal with Dionysus and what he represents in the light of traditional Greek ways of running the human community.

The most significant of these responses is that of Pentheus, the king. On the surface, he is acting like a traditional tragic hero, accepting responsibility for protecting the city in the face of an obvious political crisis (all the women out of town raising havoc among the local villages, tearing cattle apart, and so on) and acting decisively to restore order. But we quickly sense that Pentheus, unlike, say, Oedipus or Achilles (or even Creon in *Antigone*, for that matter), has complex inner problems (especially concerning sexuality), so that his responses to the crisis (all that talk of prisons, soldiers, massacres, and so forth, along with his constant military escort, his fascination with Dionysus' appearance, especially the obsession with his hair) come across more as a psychological response to certain personal inadequacies or inner pressures (things he'd sooner not think about or is even unaware of in himself) than a genuine desire to do the right thing for the city or to assert a self-confident sense of his own greatness based upon a past record of achievement. This aspect of the play makes it the most psychologically compelling of all the Greek tragedies, and dealing with this psychological dimension is obviously essential in any coherent evaluation of the play.

Finally (to conclude this short list of obvious features), the actions of this play are brutally destructive: the palace is destroyed, the major characters are all punished horribly by an omnipotent god who is supremely confident about his powers and (much of the time) superbly contemptuous of the human beings he is dealing with (the references to the enigmatic smile of Dionysus are important here). In his distribution of punishments, Dionysus seems to refuse to consider that some of those he is punishing so dreadfully made some attempt to accept his worship and to persuade others to do the same. At the end of the play Thebes (the oldest city in Greek mythology, the place where the Greek race originated, as the play reminds us) is in ruins, its ruling family (the origin of the people of Thebes) is finished, as Dionysus and his followers sweep off to the next Greek city (presumably to re-enact what we have just seen). The final image we are left with is the scattered parts of Pentheus' body (the only unburied corpse in Greek tragedy, as Jan Kott reminds us), and the memory of the fact that, under the god's forceful control, his mother ripped him apart and (perhaps) ate some of him. The only one left unshocked by what happens in Dionysus' version of a deserved "punishment" is Dionysus himself, who throughout the play seems to be enjoying himself immensely (the marked silence of the Chorus near the end suggests that even they may wondering just what their leader has done in the service of the religion they celebrate in his name, although the significant gap in the manuscript near the end may include something to meet this point). Dionysus' statements justifying his treatment of Cadmus, Pentheus, and Agave are brutally curt and impossible to accept as a satisfactory justification for what has happened.

What makes this brutality all the worse is that Dionysus' treatment of human beings robs them of their dignity. Greek tragedy is, of course, no stranger to excessively harsh treatment of human beings by malevolent gods (Oedipus being the supreme example), but such treatment does not usually remove from the main characters a sense of their own heroic worth as they try to cope--in fact, confronting that heroic magnificence in the face of a hostile or unpredictable or unknown (but ultimately destructive) divine presence is the most important part of the imaginative wonder we experience in reading a great deal of Greek literature, from the *Iliad* onwards.

But in *The Bacchae* such heroic worth is hard to find, simply because so many major characters are either merely silly (like Tiresias and Cadmus) or have no control over what they are doing (like Pentheus or Agave)--lacking power over themselves, they are not free to make the decisions through which the values of heroic self-assertiveness manifest themselves. In that sense, they are very different from earlier heroic figures, who may well live in a fatalistic universe ruled by mysterious and hostile irrational powers but who never abandon the essence of their individual greatness: the freedom to assert their value in the face of such a fate. For such self-assertion (no matter how personally disastrous) to have value (that is, to manifest some human qualities worthy of our admiration and respect), we must see it as something freely willed, something undertaken deliberately in the face of other options. Such freedom Pentheus does not have, because he is in the grip of inner compulsions which do not enable him to make independent choices. If there is a necessary connection between his actions and his fate, that connection stems from his unconscious psychological weakness rather than from his conscious heroic assertiveness, pubic-spiritedness, or courage. This, it strikes me, is a crucial point (to which I shall return later on).

Let us now turn to some of the ways interpreters have encouraged us to understand these (and other) matters.

The Bacchae *as a Punishment for Impiety*

One easy way to shape the events of the play is to see it as a relatively un-problematic morality story whose main trust is divine punishment against Pentheus and Thebes for their refusal to accept the godhead of Dionysus (this, of course, is Dionysus' view). Taken at the most simplistic level, the brutality in the play might thus be seen as justification for evil behaviour or heresy: Pentheus and Agave act badly, they should have known better than to disrespect the divine (as the chorus repeatedly points out), and they earn their punishment, since people ought to respect and obey and worship the gods (or God).

Such a response is, of course, drastically oversimple, but it is also very reassuring, since it enables us to place any potential difficulties we might have in exploring some disturbing complexities (like the astonishingly brutal and irrational ending--so disproportionately savage) into a comfortably familiar moral rubric. In fact, such easy moralizing is a common feature of many interpretations of Greek works (especially tragedies) offered by those who do not wish to face up to some unsettling possibilities (so Oedipus deservedly suffers because he commits sin or has too quick a temper, the destruction of Troy--as presented in the *Iliad*--is just, because Paris shouldn't have run off with Helen, and so on). This tendency, it strikes me, though very common, is essentially a reflex response of, among others, modern liberal rationalists who don't want to face up to the full ironic complexity of tragic fatalism (but that's a subject for another lecture).

The notion that we are witnessing some acceptable form of divine justice here is surely stained once we consider the horrific and all-encompassing nature of that punishment--the destruction of an ancient centre of civilization, the degradation, self-abasement, and horrific death of the hero, the killing of a son by his mother, and extreme punishments handed out to all, no matter how they respond to the arrival of the god, combined with the pleasure the god takes in inflicting such destruction on human civilization and the inadequacy of his explanation. All these bring out strongly the irrationality, even the insanity, of Dionysus' "justice." So it becomes difficult, I think, to force the play into a comfortably rational shape, if by that we mean that it endorses some easy moral belief that evil is, more or less, punishment for sin.

A more sophisticated (and certainly more interesting) version of this approach to the play looks at Dionysus, not simply as a foreign god, but as the embodiment of certain aspects of human experience, as a symbol for the irrational, communal excitement, bonding, power, joy, intoxication, and excess which all too often get lost in the careful life of the city, governed by habit, rules, laws, and responsibilities. This approach to the play stresses the fact that Thebes has lost touch with those irrational energizing unconscious powers of life and, in Agave's and Pentheus' refusal to acknowledge the divinity of Dionysus, created a situation where these powers (which cannot be forever denied) simply break out with disastrous consequences. If that doesn't carry an explicit moral, at least it serves as a cautionary tale.

This view has a good deal to recommend it, particularly in the figure of Pentheus, who is clearly striving throughout much of the play to repress hidden irrational desires and to deal with a fascination with and horror of those desires. He seeks to cope by encasing everything, including himself, inside metal (chains or armour) and by lashing out with male force (soldiers and commands), trying to impose a sense of external order on something which repels and attracts him, something which is obviously connected to his buried feelings about sexuality, an issue to which he keeps returning obsessively (whether in connection with Dionysus or the Bacchic women). However else we see Pentheus, it is not difficult to observe in him a person who is incapable of uniting his conscious sense of who he is as a king (political leader) with his unconscious repressed awareness of himself as an emotional (and especially a sexual) being with hidden and unfulfilled desires (a point brought out emphatically by the male-female polarity in the conflict).

This aspect of the play is also strongly brought out by the obvious similarities between Pentheus and Dionysus--both young men from the same family. It's not difficult to make the case that, in a sense, in those central confrontations between the two characters, Pentheus is having to deal with a part of himself, a part that he doesn't recognize as his (or doesn't want to). The fact that Dionysus was born in Thebes underscores this point--he may have been long absent, but he is by birth as much a part of Thebes as Pentheus (both are grandsons of Cadmus). So Pentheus' rejection of Dionysus is a rejection of him as a close family member (part of himself), as well as a rejection of his divinity. And Dionysus' confident manipulation of Pentheus evokes a strong sense that he is very much at home in Pentheus' psyche and understands well just how ineffectual all those external controls Pentheus is relying on are going to be once he (Dionysus) starts playing to those repressed desires Pentheus harbours.

The play also links the music central to Dionysian ritual with the very earliest development of the Olympian gods (Zeus' birth), so there's a sense here that what Dionysus celebrates is a fixed and divinely ordained part of the scheme of things, no matter how much some people may have forgotten or never known that.

It's possible, on this view, to argue that Dionysus is initially seeking some synthesis in Thebes, some reinvigoration of the city by the introduction and acceptance of his rituals (hence to restore life to a more appropriate balance), with initially no particularly destructive intent, but that he changes his mind in the face of Pentheus' intransigence. Dionysus, after all, volunteers to bring the women back into the city, without violence, an offer which suggests that some compromise may be possible. Only after Pentheus typically rejects the offer (or ignores it), does Dionysus then tempt Pentheus out into the mountains to his death. This moment when Dionysus makes his offer and Pentheus rejects it is a particularly interesting one, suggesting as it does that Pentheus may be unwilling to compromise *because* he wants to see something illegal, sexual, naughty--he doesn't want to accommodate himself to it (by having the women back in the city), but to enjoy it all the more because it offends him--the urge to enjoy the *frisson* of a voyeur overcomes any desire to understand and adjust--there would be no delight in seeing the women dance if that was legal, part of everyday life (given this point, just what he might be doing sitting under the trees in silence as he watches the Bacchic women invites some imaginative exploration). So we might see the destruction of Pentheus as the self-immolation of a man too afraid of his inner self to address it maturely and too fascinated with it to repress it successfully.

However, there are some difficulties with this line of interpretation. Apart from the fact that Dionysus gives very little indication of a genuine intent to harmonize his religion with Greek political life (given how well he understands Pentheus, that offer mentioned above may be just one more psychological deception, a preparation for what he has had in mind all along, the total humiliation and meaningless destruction of Pentheus), the play offers us no sense that a harmonious synthesis with what Thebes has become and the new religion of Dionysus is possible. If it offered us that, then it might be easier to see Pentheus' destruction as a particular instance of one badly fractured personality. But instead the play holds up for ridicule those Thebans who do seek to worship Dionysus (Tiresias and Cadmus) and subjects the women who have gone up into the mountains to the most horrific punishments.

In addition, the play stresses the uncivil and anti-civil actions required and encouraged by Dionysian rituals (especially the abandoning and kidnapping of children, the destruction of domestic animals, and so on--culminating in the most anti-civil action of all, the mother's destruction of her child, an act which, more than any other, violates the basic reason for the community's existence). Given what this play shows us, it is difficult to believe that a reconciliation between Dionysian religion and civil life is possible. And if that is not available, then what sort of cautionary tale are we being offered here? What exactly are we, as spectators, supposed to take away from this in the way of closure?

The Bacchae *as an Indictment of Dionysian Religion*

Given this last point, it is not difficult to see why some interpreters have viewed this play as an indictment of religion because of its hostility to the survival of the community, on the ground that religion (as depicted by Dionysus and his followers) is the basis for the irrational destructiveness which threatens and ultimately overthrows the well-ordered city in an orgy of cruel excess. On this view, the play is a cautionary tale about the dangers of religious superstitions.

This approach naturally makes a good deal of the way in which the play always links the benefits of Dionysian religion, its value as a beautiful, creative celebration, with destructiveness, with anti-political or extra-polit-ical activities, and, from time to time, with a sense of passive resignation: human life is really not worth much, but at least, thanks to Dionysus, we have wine, which enables us to forget our troubles, so we should worship the god who makes it possible for us to get drunk and not strive to be anything better than we are. And in the Dionysian celebrations we can for-get our individual cares, responsibilities, and laws and give free rein to our inhibitions--a sure way to undermine the things most essential to human well being and happiness, namely, the security of a well-governed city and the rational powers of the human mind to make things better (or at least stop them from getting worse).

If we focus exclusively upon these features of the play, then it's not difficult to sense how many might see it as a scathing attack on popular superstitions, particularly those which generate enthusiasm through mass hysteria and crowd violence in the face of calmer, more traditional controls (and self-control). But there are difficulties in pushing this interpretative possibility too far.

The major obstacle here, of course, is the figure of Pentheus himself. As the political ruler of Thebes, he embodies the nature and value of the civic authority threatened by Dionysian excess. And whatever we might like to say about Pentheus, he is hardly someone in whom we might celebrate the enduring values of civilized and just political life (for reasons mentioned above in the previous section). Quite the reverse--he seems as much a threat to what is valuable in civic life as Dionysus (although, of course, he is un-aware of that).

In addition, the traditional values of Thebes are, in the figures of Tiresias and especially Cadmus, exposed as silly, grotesque, and self-serving. They want to dance to the music but travel there in a chariot. Cadmus seems particularly keen that his family's status will be improved if people think his daughter has given birth to a god (whether it's true or not). Their combined physical decrepitude (the blind leading the lame) is an eloquent physical symbol of the extent to which the long traditions they represent have become enfeebled (and, as I mentioned earlier, no two mythological characters in Greek literature carry more solemn weight, from the *Odyssey* onward, than these two, so treating them this way is a bit like making, say, George Washington an anxious, neurotic, and selfish coward in a retelling of Valley Forge).

One would think that, if the main point of the play is to expose the savagery of religious superstition as a danger to civic order or peaceful political life, then the political order would be presented as something more valuable, more worth preserving than it is here. After all, whatever feelings of horror and sympathetic pathos we may feel at Pentheus' destruction, there is no sense that he carries an inherent dignity and redeeming value which is sacrificed with him (other than his presence as a confused, suffering, inadequate human being). The same applies Tiresias and Cadmus and Agave.

The Bacchae *as a Choice of Nightmares*

A more persuasive and inclusive approach to the play, it strikes me, builds on the strengths of the previously mentioned alternatives, refusing to see it as endorsing one side of the dichotomy against the other (Pentheus and Thebes or Dionysus and the Bacchants) and instead exploring the play as a particularly despairing vision of the destructiveness inherent in the ambiguities of human existence, contradictions which simply cannot be reconciled into some harmonious creative whole. Rather than being a cautionary tale, the play is a passionate vision of total despair.

This approach would stress that, indeed, the vision of political and traditional life of Thebes sees it as hopeless silly, insecure, and shallow, built on no confident sense of justice--something that has run out of a creative energizing faith in itself (hence the reflex reliance on power). Those who embody ancient traditions (Cadmus and Tiresias) have become self-serving caricatures of what they used to be. The traditional source of political leadership and justice (the king, Pentheus) is radically uncertain of his identity, wracked with inner complexities which control his actions, and thus without any confident self-assertiveness or sense of responsibility for the sake of the community. The considerable power he exercises hence comes to be used primarily to protect himself against his own inner insecurities. No wonder he is much more more concerned with confinement and slaughter than he is with justice--he's fighting against his own inner desires which (as mentioned above) attract and repel him.

At the same time, his polar opposite, Dionysus, for all the supreme self-confidence he displays, is a malevolent destroyer. The gifts he brings are considerable, but they are not compatible with civilized human achievement (at least not as this play presents them)--they not merely challenge existing traditions; they also completely obliterate those who stand in their way. And they do this, not in the name of some workable political or communal alternative, but for the sake of mass ecstatic frenzy outside the traditional community and drunken oblivion within it.

If we remember that the central concern of the human community in Greek literature is justice--the best arrangement whereby human beings can live and prosper together as citizens of a political unit, then Pentheus and Dionysus both bring out the extent to which justice has disappeared. Pentheus is concerned only with power in the shoring up of his own inadequate personality; Dionysus is concerned only with ecstatic release in a mass frenzy and the total destruction of those who do not immediately comply--all in order to convert civic life into an irrational manifestation of belief in what he represents.

Incidentally, in considering the importance of this idea of justice, we should not be too quick to accept the Chorus' frequent invocations of what they call justice as the "message" of the play or as the point of view the author is hoping we'll accept. It's true the Chorus frequently sings of justice, but a close view of what they mean by the term stresses their irrational sense of the term: for them justice is a god-given right to oppress one's enemies or a willed refusal to do anything more than passively accept the given conditions of life. These two options, I would suggest, remove from the term justice any central concern with the difficult struggle to establish fairness in the community and repetitively insist upon the extent to which the worship of Dionysus, as defined here, runs directly counter to the major concern of Greek political life.

The play offers no suggestion that a reconciliation between these two cousins is possible. Human experience is radically split into two diametrically opposed and inherently incomplete possibilities. When they come together, destruction of civilization results--a horror in which there is no room for human beings to manifest the slightest individual dignity and hence assert some human values in their suffering (in fact, their individuality is taken away from them before they die, so that they become objects of mockery or pathos). So it doesn't matter which side one chooses to align oneself with, Dionysus or Pentheus, the end result is the same. There is no moral lesson to be learned--that's simply the way the world works.

Jan Kott in a remarkably interesting essay drew a fruitful parallel between *The Bacchae* and Conrad's famous story *Heart of Darkness*, in which (to simplify a very complex fiction and Kott's remarks on it) human experience is presented to us as offering two irreconcilable possibilities--the European life on the surface (with its stress on political power, suppression of nature, urban bureaucratic rationality, and ignorance of the inner life) and African life lived from the heart (with its stress on passion, dancing, mass movement, and cannibalism, in the prehistoric wilderness of the jungle). Conrad's tale explores (among other things) the mutual destruction which occurs when these two ways of life (or aspects of life) collide, and it offers us no hope for some harmonious reconciliation (either politically or psychologically). The experience of these possibilities leaves Marlowe with the cryptic final comment that life is, in effect, a "choice of nightmares"--one can stay on the surface or move into the darkness, but either way life is inherently unfulfilled. Someone who, like Kurtz, tries to experience both as fully as possible is left in self-destructive despair ("The horror! The horror!").

Kott's parallel, it strikes me, is very illuminating, because it does justice to the full power of Euripides' play--especially the savage vision of despair at the end, which we might like to mute by imposing on it some more comfortable moral "lesson," but which is much too powerful to be contained by such a confining and neat interpretative scheme.

Thinking about the parallels between these two stories, I am struck by how much more despairing Euripides' tale is than Conrad's. For in Conrad's story, the two ways of life are widely separated geographically, and there's a sense that so long as that separation remains, the European civilization will continue, content on the surface and economically prosperous in its ignorant idealism (although Marlowe senses it is slowly dying). And in that story we also have the figure of Marlowe as someone who, if he has not reconciled the white and the black, has adopted a meditative stance towards the paradoxes of his experience and finds some purpose in sailing back and forth between them and in telling his story. But in Euripides' play there is no similar sense--the worlds of Dionysus and Pentheus are inevitably colliding, with more examples to follow, and we have no final consolation in a Marlowe-like figure. Instead we have the scattered bits of Pentheus, all that remains of Thebes and its royal family.

A Note on the Historical Context

Those who like to anchor their interpretations on details of historical context (not a procedure I personally recommend for reasons there is not time to go into here, but a popular method of proceeding nonetheless) will find plenty of potentially useful supporting detail for the final suggestions given above. Let me briefly mention a few.

The Bacchae is one of Euripides' very last works (unperformed in his life, with the manuscript discovered at his death), written when the aging writer had turned his back on Greece and moved to Macedon (around 408 BC) shortly before his death, perhaps bitter because he had never achieved the highest success as a tragedian in Athens or in his frustration at Athenian political life. At this time the long drawn-out insanity of the Peloponnesian War was in its final stages, and its destructive effects on the highest Greek (especially Athenian) achievements were plain for all to see, as the possibilities for a just communal political life among the Greek city-states and within particular states had foundered on greed, self-interest, mass killings,

Persian money, the corruption or abandonment of traditional ways, and political incompetence (in short, on the disappearance of justice).

The sense that in this war the Greeks were in the grip of some mass self-destructive insanity which weak traditional political structures and shallow personalities were inadequate to deal with was by no means confined to Euripides (if that is how we read his play)--there is strong corroboration in, among other texts, the apocalyptic ending of the *Clouds* and, of course, throughout Thucydides.

The Mythological Framework: Some Comments

The above interpretative suggestions are underscored by the remarkably rich treatment of a number of important Greek myths throughout the play. These highlight the tensions between the eastern (barbarian) and Greek responses to life and to the divine and suggest by the end that the Greek way has been overcome and banished. There may well be a sense that whatever it was which made Greece special (in contrast to the barbarians), the Greek "experiment," if you will, has ended. Without going into great detail, let me suggest some of the ways in which the mythic content of the play and the discussion of how one understands myth help to illuminate this play's despairing vision.

Central to *The Bacchae* is the family of Cadmus. The play reminds us early on that Cadmus came from Asia (from Sidon) and created the Greek race by sowing the dragon's teeth which produced the first Greeks (the Cadmeians)--an event which is referred to more than once. Cadmus also married Harmonia, an immortal, in a celebration which (like the similar union of Achilles' parents, Peleus and Thetis) symbolizes the possibility of a harmonious relationship between the human and the divine as the creative basis for the just community (of the sort we see dramatically symbolized at the end of Aeschylus' *Oresteia*).

The play forces us to examine the destruction of this earlier harmony between gods and men and hence of the political and communal ideal which it endorses. Dionysus, an eastern god (or a god bringing with him a different relationship to the divine) is interested in submission, ecstatic revelry, and drink. Those who do not at once celebrate this vision of divinity are subjected to harsh, instant, irrational punishment for disobedience. And the penalty he inflicts here--the killing of a child by his mother and the banishment of the royal family into barbarian lands (a significant contrast to the *Oresteia*, where the killing of a mother by the son helps to establish human justice under divine auspices in the polis)--marks an end to whatever Greek Thebes was all about to begin with. The barbarian East, where Cadmus originally came from, has triumphed.

There may even be a sense here in the *Bacchae* that the experiment was doomed from the start. That, at any rate, is one construction one can put on the strong emphasis given in this play to an eastern vision of Zeus, a Zeus who, as E. R. Dodds points out (84), seems far more like Dionysus than the traditional Greek notion of Zeus (especially in all those details linking Zeus' birth to the irrationality of Dionysian revels and in Dionysus' repeated insistence that he is the son of Zeus). The emphasis on the overwhelming destructiveness of the gods (from Zeus' lighting bolt which kills Semele to the tearing apart of Actaeon, as well as Dionysus' conduct in the play) tends constantly to undercut any sense that some sort of harmonious cooperation between humans and the divine, some arrangement which gives human beings a chance to manifest their worth in a traditionally Greek way, is possible.

But if this play is exploring such a despairing vision, it offers us the sense that part of the problem is the loss of human participation in the original arrangement. In the *Bacchae*, we witness the deterioration of the human capacity to accept the mystery of divine mythology as a vitalizing and creative political presence--and the enduring value of the link between the human and the divine celebrated in the marriage of Cadmus and Harmonia depends upon that more than anything else.

Here, however, Cadmus' children refuse to enter the world of religious myth. Semele's sisters see her story as a convenient lie to excuse her sexual promiscuity with some man, and Pentheus is far too concerned with secular power and his own inadequacies to entertain a truly religious thought. Cadmus sees religion primarily as a way of making his family more important (and thus protecting himself). None of them displays any true reverence for the mysteries of life passed down to them (in this respect, one might note the significant differences between them and, say, Oedipus in *Oedipus the King*).

The most interesting figure in connection with this attitude to mythology is Tiresias, traditionally a mediator between divine wisdom and limited human understanding. Here he seems more concerned to rationalize Dionysus away, rather than to accept him as a particular, immediate, and mysterious religious experience. Hence, he can subject the myth of Dionysus' birth from the thigh of Zeus to rational analysis (Dodds has some excellent comments on this point on 91). There may well be some satiric intent in this presentation of Tiresias (maybe), but, beyond the most immediate satire, there may also be a sense that this most venerable of religious sensibilities has degenerated (or, if that is too strong, changed) into a new form of thinking which makes religious belief at least difficult and at most ridiculous.

Depending on the construction one puts upon the attitude to mythology in the *Bacchae*, one might offer a variety of interpretative possibilities concerning Euripides' final word on Greek traditions, from lament to satire. My own view is that the play is not taking sides, but rather, as I have mentioned, exploring a passionate sense of despair at what has happened and what the future holds. With one eye on the philosophical revolution which, in the figures of Socrates and Plato, is going to attempt to redefine the basis of the good life, we can understand why Nietzsche (in *The Birth of Tragedy*) sees Euripides and Socrates as soul mates, but we do not have to go that far. The play evokes a terrible sense of something coming to an end (the exile of Cadmus and Harmonia and the end of Greek Thebes)--and it invites speculation about what now happens to the human community in the face of the triumph of Dionysian irrationality and destruction.

Works Cited

E. R. Dodds, editor. *Euripides Bacchae.* Second Edition. Oxford: Clarendon Press, 1977.

Jan Kott. *The Eating of the Gods: An Interpretation of Greek Tragedy.* NY: Random House, 1974.

BAKXAI

BACCHAE

ΤΑ ΤΟΥ ΔΡΑΜΑΤΟΣ ΠΡΟΣΩΠΑ

ΔΙΟΝΥΣΟΣ

ΤΕΙΡΕΣΙΑΣ

ΚΑΔΜΟΣ

ΠΕΝΘΕΥΣ

ΑΓΑΥΗ

ΑΓΓΕΛΟΣ

ΕΤΕΡΟΣ ΑΓΓΕΛΟΣ

ΧΟΡΟΣ

ΘΕΡΑΠΩΝ

DRAMATIS PERSONAE

DIONYSUS: divine son of Zeus and Semele, also
called Bromius or Bacchus.

TIRESIAS: an old blind prophet

CADMUS: grandfather of both Dionysus and Pentheus, an old man

PENTHEUS: young king of Thebes, grandson of Cadmus, cousin of
Dionysus

AGAVE: mother of Pentheus, daughter of Cadmus, sister of Semele

FIRST MESSENGER: a cattle herder

SECOND MESSENGER: an attendant on Pentheus

CHORUS OF BACCHAE: worshippers of Dionysus who have followed
him from Asia.

SOLDIERS and ATTENDANTS around Pentheus

3

Βάκχαι

ΔΙΟΝΥΣΟΣ
  ἥκω Διὸς παῖς τήνδε Θηβαίων χθόνα
  Διόνυσος, ὃν τίκτει ποθ' ἡ Κάδμου κόρη
  Σεμέλη λοχευθεῖσ' ἀστραπηφόρῳ πυρί·
  μορφὴν δ' ἀμείψας ἐκ θεοῦ βροτησίαν
  πάρειμι Δίρκης νάματ' Ἰσμηνοῦ θ' ὕδωρ.   5
  ὁρῶ δὲ μητρὸς μνῆμα τῆς κεραυνίας
  τόδ' ἐγγὺς οἴκων καὶ δόμων ἐρείπια
  τυφόμενα Δίου πυρὸς ἔτι ζῶσαν φλόγα,
  ἀθάνατον Ἥρας μητέρ' εἰς ἐμὴν ὕβριν.
  αἰνῶ δὲ Κάδμον, ἄβατον ὃς πέδον τόδε   10
  τίθησι, θυγατρὸς σηκόν· ἀμπέλου δέ νιν
  πέριξ ἐγὼ 'κάλυψα βοτρυώδει χλόῃ.
  λιπὼν δὲ Λυδῶν τοὺς πολυχρύσους γύας
  Φρυγῶν τε, Περσῶν θ' ἡλιοβλήτους πλάκας
  Βάκτριά τε τείχη τήν τε δύσχιμον χθόνα   15
  Μήδων ἐπελθὼν Ἀραβίαν τ' εὐδαίμονα
  Ἀσίαν τε πᾶσαν, ἣ παρ' ἁλμυρὰν ἅλα
  κεῖται μιγάσιν Ἕλλησι βαρβάροις θ' ὁμοῦ
  πλήρεις ἔχουσα καλλιπυργώτους πόλεις,
  ἐς τήνδε πρῶτον ἦλθον Ἑλλήνων πόλιν,   20
  τἀκεῖ χορεύσας καὶ καταστήσας ἐμὰς
  τελετάς, ἵν' εἴην ἐμφανὴς δαίμων βροτοῖς.
  πρώτας δὲ Θήβας τῆσδε γῆς Ἑλληνίδος
  ἀνωλόλυξα, νεβρίδ' ἐξάψας χροὸς
  θύρσον τε δοὺς ἐς χεῖρα, κίσσινον βέλος·   25
  ἐπεί μ' ἀδελφαὶ μητρός, ἃς ἥκιστα χρῆν,

4

Bacchae

SCENE: *The Greek city of Thebes, outside the royal palace. Dionysus, appearing as young man, is alone, with the palace behind him, its main doors facing the audience. He speaks directly to the audience*

DIONYSUS

    I've arrived here in the land of Thebes,
    I, Dionysus, son of Zeus, born to him
    from Semele, Cadmus' daughter, delivered
    by a fiery midwife—Zeus' lightning flash.[1]
    Yes, I've changed my form from god to human,
    appearing here at these streams of Dirce,
    the waters of Ismarus. I see my mother's tomb—
    for she was wiped out by that lightning bolt.
    It's there, by the palace, with that rubble,
    the remnants of her house, still smoldering
    from Zeus' living fire—Hera's undying outrage
    against my mother. But I praise Cadmus.   [10]
    He's made his daughter's shrine a sacred place.
    I have myself completely covered it
    with leafy shoots of grape-bearing vines.
    I've left the fabulously wealthy East,
    lands of Lydians and Phrygians,
    Persia's sun-drenched plains, walled towns in Bactria.
    I've moved across the bleak lands of the Medes,
    through rich Arabia, all Asian lands,
    along the salt-sea coast, through those towns
    with their beautifully constructed towers,
    full of barbarians and Greeks all intermingled.
    Now I've come to Thebes, city of Greeks,   [20]
    only after I've set those eastern lands
    dancing in the mysteries I established,
    making known to men my own divinity.
    Thebes is the first city of the Greeks
    where I've roused people to shout out my cries,
    with this deerskin draped around my body,
    this ivy spear, a thyrsus, in my hand.[2]
    For my mother's sisters have acted badly,
    something they, of all people, should avoid.

Διόνυσον οὐκ ἔφασκον ἐκφῦναι Διός,

Σεμέλην δὲ νυμφευθεῖσαν ἐκ θνητοῦ τινος

ἐς Ζῆν᾽ ἀναφέρειν τὴν ἁμαρτίαν λέχους,

Κάδμου σοφίσμαθ᾽, ὧν νιν οὕνεκα κτανεῖν   30

Ζῆν᾽ ἐξεκαυχῶνθ᾽, ὅτι γάμους ἐψεύσατο.

τοιγάρ νιν αὐτὰς ἐκ δόμων ᾤστρησ᾽ ἐγὼ

μανίαις, ὄρος δ᾽ οἰκοῦσι παράκοποι φρενῶν·

σκευήν τ᾽ ἔχειν ἠνάγκασ᾽ ὀργίων ἐμῶν,

καὶ πᾶν τὸ θῆλυ σπέρμα Καδμείων, ὅσαι   35

γυναῖκες ἦσαν, ἐξέμηνα δωμάτων·

ὁμοῦ δὲ Κάδμου παισὶν ἀναμεμειγμέναι

χλωραῖς ὑπ᾽ ἐλάταις ἀνορόφοις ἧνται πέτραις.

δεῖ γὰρ πόλιν τήνδ᾽ ἐκμαθεῖν, κεἰ μὴ θέλει,

ἀτέλεστον οὖσαν τῶν ἐμῶν βακχευμάτων,   40

Σεμέλης τε μητρὸς ἀπολογήσασθαί μ᾽ ὕπερ

φανέντα θνητοῖς δαίμον᾽ ὃν τίκτει Διί.

Κάδμος μὲν οὖν γέρας τε καὶ τυραννίδα

Πενθεῖ δίδωσι θυγατρὸς ἐκπεφυκότι,

ὃς θεομαχεῖ τὰ κατ᾽ ἐμὲ καὶ σπονδῶν ἄπο   45

ὠθεῖ μ᾽, ἐν εὐχαῖς τ᾽ οὐδαμοῦ μνείαν ἔχει.

ὧν οὕνεκ᾽ αὐτῷ θεὸς γεγὼς ἐνδείξομαι

πᾶσίν τε Θηβαίοισιν. ἐς δ᾽ ἄλλην χθόνα,

τἀνθένδε θέμενος εὖ, μεταστήσω πόδα,

δεικνὺς ἐμαυτόν· ἢν δὲ Θηβαίων πόλις   50

ὀργῇ σὺν ὅπλοις ἐξ ὄρους βάκχας ἄγειν

ζητῇ, ξυνάψω μαινάσι στρατηλατῶν.

ὧν οὕνεκ᾽ εἶδος θνητὸν ἀλλάξας ἔχω

μορφήν τ᾽ ἐμὴν μετέβαλον εἰς ἀνδρὸς φύσιν.

6

They boasted aloud that I, Dionysus,
was no child of Zeus, claiming Semele,
once she was pregnant by some mortal man,
attributed her bad luck in bed to Zeus,
a story made up (they said) to trick Cadmus.   [30]
Those sisters state that's why Zeus killed her,
because she lied about the man she'd slept with.
So I've driven those women from their homes
in a frenzy—they now live in the mountains,
out of their minds. I've made them put on costumes,
outfits appropriate for my mysteries.
All Theban offspring—or, at least, all women—
I've driven in a crazed fit from their homes.
Now they sit out there among the rocks,
underneath green pine trees, no roof overhead,
Cadmus' daughters in their company as well.
For this city has to learn, though against its will,
that it has yet to be initiated
into my Dionysian rites. Here I plead   [40]
the cause of my own mother, Semele,
appearing as a god to mortal men,
the one she bore to Zeus. Now Cadmus,
the old king, has just transferred his power,
his royal authority, to Pentheus,
his daughter's son, who, in my case at least,
fights against the gods, prohibiting me
all sacrificial offerings. When he prays,
he chooses to ignore me. For this neglect
I'll demonstrate to him, to all in Thebes,
that I was born a god. Once these things here
have been made right, I'll move on somewhere else,
to some other land, revealing who I am.
But if Thebans in this city, in their anger,   [50]
try to make those Bacchic women leave,
to drive them from the mountains forcibly,
then I, commander of these Maenads,
will fight them.3 That's why I've transformed myself,
assumed a mortal shape, altered my looks,
so I resemble any human being.

7

ἀλλ᾽, ὦ λιποῦσαι Τμῶλον ἔρυμα Λυδίας,   55
θίασος ἐμός, γυναῖκες, ἃς ἐκ βαρβάρων
ἐκόμισα παρέδρους καὶ ξυνεμπόρους ἐμοί,
αἴρεσθε τἀπιχώρι᾽ ἐν πόλει Φρυγῶν
τύμπανα, Ῥέας τε μητρὸς ἐμά θ᾽ εὑρήματα,
βασίλειά τ᾽ ἀμφὶ δώματ᾽ ἐλθοῦσαι τάδε   60
κτυπεῖτε Πενθέως, ὡς ὁρᾷ Κάδμου πόλις.
ἐγὼ δὲ βάκχαις, ἐς Κιθαιρῶνος πτυχὰς
ἐλθὼν ἵν᾽ εἰσί, συμμετασχήσω χορῶν.

ΧΟΡΟΣ
    Ἀσίας ἀπὸ γᾶς
    ἱερὸν Τμῶλον ἀμείψασα θοάζω   65
    Βρομίῳ πόνον ἡδὺν
    κάματόν τ᾽ εὐκάματον, Βάκ-
    χιον εὐαζομένα.

— τίς ὁδῷ τίς ὁδῷ; τίς;
    μελάθροις ἔκτοπος ἔστω, στόμα τ᾽ εὔφη-
    μον ἅπας ἐξοσιούσθω·   70
    τὰ νομισθέντα γὰρ αἰεὶ
    Διόνυσον ὑμνήσω.

— ὦ
    μάκαρ, ὅστις εὐδαίμων
    τελετὰς θεῶν εἰδὼς

[Enter the Chorus of Bacchae, dressed in ritual deerskin, carrying small drums like tambourines]

> But you there, you women who've left Tmolus,
> backbone of Lydia, my band of worshippers,
> whom I've led here from barbarian lands,
> my comrades on the road and when we rest,
> take up your drums, those instruments of yours
> from Phrygian cities, first invented
> by mother Rhea and myself. Move round here,
> beat those drums by Pentheus' palace,   [60]
> let Cadmus' city see you, while I go,
> in person, to the clefts of Mount Cithaeron,
> to my Bacchae, to join their dancing.4

[Exit Dionysus]

CHORUS *[singing and dancing]*

FIRST VOICE

> From Asia, from sacred Tmolus
> I've come to dance,
> to move swiftly in my dance—
> for Bromius—
> sweet and easy task,
> to cry out in celebration,
> hailing great god Bacchus.5

SECOND VOICE

> Who's in the street? Who's there? Who?
> Let him stay inside
> out of our way.
> Let every mouth be pure,   [70]
> completely holy,
> speak no profanities.
> In my hymn I celebrate
> our old eternal custom,
> hailing Dionysus.

THIRD VOICE

> O blessed is the man,
> the fortunate man who knows
> the rituals of the gods,

9

βιοτὰν ἁγιστεύει καὶ
θιασεύεται ψυχὰν   75
ἐν ὄρεσσι βακχεύων
ὁσίοις καθαρμοῖσιν,
τά τε ματρὸς μεγάλας ὄρ-
για Κυβέλας θεμιτεύων,
ἀνὰ θύρσον τε τινάσσων,   80
κισσῷ τε στεφανωθεὶς
Διόνυσον θεραπεύει.

— ἴτε βάκχαι, ἴτε βάκχαι,
Βρόμιον παῖδα θεὸν θεοῦ
Διόνυσον κατάγουσαι   85
Φρυγίων ἐξ ὀρέων Ἑλ-
λάδος εἰς εὐρυχόρους ἀ-
γυιάς, τὸν Βρόμιον·

— ὅν
ποτ᾽ ἔχουσ᾽ ἐν ὠδίνων
λοχίαις ἀνάγκαισι
πταμένας Διὸς βροντᾶς νη-   90
δύος ἔκβολον μάτηρ
ἔτεκεν, λιποῦσ᾽ αἰῶ-
να κεραυνίῳ πληγᾷ·
λοχίοις δ᾽ αὐτίκα νιν δέ-
ξατο θαλάμαις Κρονίδας Ζεύς,   95
κατὰ μηρῷ δὲ καλύψας
χρυσέαισιν συνερείδει
περόναις κρυπτὸν ἀφ᾽ Ἥρας.

— ἔτεκεν δ᾽, ἁνίκα Μοῖραι
τέλεσαν, ταυρόκερων θεὸν   100
στεφάνωσέν τε δρακόντων
στεφάνοις, ἔνθεν ἄγραν θη-
ροτρόφον μαινάδες ἀμφι-
βάλλονται πλοκάμοις.

— ὦ Σεμέλας τροφοὶ Θῆ-   105
βαι, στεφανοῦσθε κισσῷ·

10

who leads a pious life,
whose spirit merges
with these Bacchic celebrations,
frenzied dancing in the mountains,
our purifying rites—
one who reveres these mysteries
from Cybele, our great mother,
who, waving the thyrsus,   [80]
forehead crowned with ivy,
serves Dionysus.

FOURTH VOICE

On Bacchae! Bacchae, move!
Bring home Bromius, our god,
son of god, great Dionysus,
from Phrygian mountains
to spacious roads of Greece—
Hail Bromius!

FIFTH VOICE

His mother dropped him early,
as her womb, in forceful birth pangs,
was struck by Zeus' flying lightning bolt,   [90]
a blast which took her life.
Then Zeus, son of Cronos,
at once hid him away
in a secret birthing chamber,
buried in his thigh,
shut in with golden clasps,
concealed from Hera.

SIXTH VOICE

Fates made him perfect.
Then Zeus gave birth to him,   [100]
the god with ox's horns,
crowned with wreaths of snakes—
that's why the Maenads
twist in their hair
wild snakes they capture.

SEVENTH VOICE

O Thebes, nursemaid of Semele,
put on your ivy crown,

βρύετε βρύετε χλοήρει
μίλακι καλλικάρπῳ
καὶ καταβακχιοῦσθε δρυὸς
ἢ ἐλάτας κλάδοισι,   110
στικτῶν τ' ἐνδυτὰ νεβρίδων
στέφετε λευκοτρίχων πλοκάμων
μαλλοῖς· ἀμφὶ δὲ νάρθηκας ὑβριστὰς
ὁσιοῦσθ'· αὐτίκα γᾶ πᾶσα χορεύσει—
Βρόμιος ὅστις ἄγῃ θιάσους—   115
εἰς ὄρος εἰς ὄρος, ἔνθα μένει
θηλυγενὴς ὄχλος
ἀφ' ἱστῶν παρὰ κερκίδων τ'
οἰστρηθεὶς Διονύσῳ.

— ὦ θαλάμευμα Κουρή-   120
των ζάθεοί τε Κρήτας
Διογενέτορες ἔναυλοι,
ἔνθα τρικόρυθες ἄντροις
βυρσότονον κύκλωμα τόδε
μοι Κορύβαντες ηὗρον·   125
βακχείᾳ δ' ἀνὰ συντόνῳ
κέρασαν ἁδυβόᾳ Φρυγίων
αὐλῶν πνεύματι ματρός τε Ῥέας ἐς
χέρα θῆκαν, κτύπον εὐάσμασι Βακχᾶν·
παρὰ δὲ μαινόμενοι Σάτυροι   130
ματέρος ἐξανύσαντο θεᾶς,
ἐς δὲ χορεύματα
συνῆψαν τριετηρίδων,
αἷς χαίρει Διόνυσος.

— ἡδὺς ἐν ὄρεσιν, ὅταν ἐκ θιάσων δρομαί-   135
ων πέσῃ πεδόσε, νε-
βρίδος ἔχων ἱερὸν ἐνδυτόν, ἀγρεύων

12

flaunt your green yew,
flaunt its sweet fruit!
Consecrate yourselves to Bacchus,
with stems of oak or fir,   [110]
Dress yourselves in spotted fawn skins,
trimmed with white sheep's wool.
As you wave your thyrsus,
revere the violence it contains.
All the earth will dance at once.
Whoever leads our dancing—
that one is Bromius!
To the mountain, to the mountain,
where the pack of women waits,
all stung to frenzied madness
to leave their weaving shuttles,
goaded on by Dionysus.

EIGHTH VOICE
O you dark chambers of the Curetes,   [120]
you sacred caves in Crete,
birthplace of Zeus,
where the Corybantes in their caves,
men with triple helmets, made for me
this circle of stretched hide.[6]
In their wild ecstatic dancing,
they mixed this drum beat
with the sweet seductive tones
of flutes from Phrygia,
then gave it to mother Rhea
to beat time for the Bacchae,
when they sang in ecstasy.
Nearby, orgiastic satyrs,   [130]
in ritual worship of the mother goddess,
took that drum, then brought it
into their biennial dance,
bringing joy to Dionysus.

NINTH VOICE
He's welcome in the mountains,
when he sinks down to the ground,
after the running dance,
wrapped in holy deerskin,

αἷμα τραγοκτόνον, ὠμοφάγον χάριν, ἱέμε-
νος ἐς ὄρεα Φρύγια, Λύδι', ὁ δ' ἔξαρχος Βρόμιος,   140
εὐοῖ.

— ῥεῖ δὲ γάλακτι πέδον, ῥεῖ δ' οἴνῳ, ῥεῖ δὲ μελισσᾶν
νέκταρι.

Συρίας δ' ὡς λιβάνου κα-
πνὸν ὁ Βακχεὺς ἀνέχων   145
πυρσώδη φλόγα πεύκας
ἐκ νάρθηκος ἀίσσει
δρόμῳ καὶ χοροῖσιν
πλανάτας ἐρεθίζων
ἰαχαῖς τ' ἀναπάλλων,
τρυφερόν τε πλόκαμον εἰς αἰθέρα ῥίπτων.   150
ἅμα δ' εὐάσμασι τοιάδ' ἐπιβρέμει·
Ὦ ἴτε βάκχαι,
ὦ ἴτε βάκχαι,
Τμώλου χρυσορόου χλιδᾷ
μέλπετε τὸν Διόνυσον   155
βαρυβρόμων ὑπὸ τυμπάνων,   157
εὔια τὸν εὔιον ἀγαλλόμεναι θεὸν
ἐν Φρυγίαισι βοαῖς ἐνοπαῖσί τε,
λωτὸς ὅταν εὐκέλαδος   160
ἱερὸς ἱερὰ παίγματα βρέμῃ, σύνοχα   164
φοιτάσιν εἰς ὄρος εἰς ὄρος· ἡδομέ-   165
να δ' ἄρα, πῶλος ὅπως ἅμα ματέρι
φορβάδι, κῶλον ἄγει ταχύπουν σκιρτήμασι βάκχα.   169

14

hunting the goat's blood,
blood of the slain beast,
devouring its raw flesh with joy,
rushing off into the mountains,
in Phrygia, in Lydia, [140]
leading the dance —
Bromius — Evoë!7

ALL

The land flows with milk,
the land flows with wine,
the land flows with honey from the bees.
He holds the torch high,
our leader, the Bacchic One,
blazing flame of pine,
sweet smoke like Syrian incense,
trailing from his thyrsus.
As he dances, he runs,
here and there,
rousing the stragglers,
stirring them with his cries,
thick hair rippling in the breeze. [150]
Among the Maenads' shouts
his voice reverberates:
"On Bacchants, on!
With the glitter of Tmolus,
which flows with gold,
chant songs to Dionysus,
to the loud beat of our drums.
Celebrate the god of joy
with your own joy,
with Phrygian cries and shouts!
When sweet sacred pipes [160]
play out their rhythmic holy song,
in time to the dancing wanderers,
then to the mountains,
on, on to the mountains."
Then the bacchanalian woman
is filled with total joy —
like a foal in pasture
right beside her mother —
her swift feet skip in playful dance.

ΤΕΙΡΕΣΙΑΣ
τίς ἐν πύλαισι; Κάδμον ἐκκάλει δόμων,   170
Ἀγήνορος παῖδ᾽, ὃς πόλιν Σιδωνίαν
λιπὼν ἐπύργωσ᾽ ἄστυ Θηβαίων τόδε.
ἴτω τις, εἰσάγγελλε Τειρεσίας ὅτι
ζητεῖ νιν· οἶδε δ᾽ αὐτὸς ὧν ἥκω πέρι
ἅ τε ξυνεθέμην πρέσβυς ὢν γεραιτέρῳ,   175
θύρσους ἀνάπτειν καὶ νεβρῶν δορὰς ἔχειν
στεφανοῦν τε κρᾶτα κισσίνοις βλαστήμασιν.

ΚΑΔΜΟΣ
ὦ φίλταθ᾽, ὡς σὴν γῆρυν ᾐσθόμην κλύων
σοφὴν σοφοῦ παρ᾽ ἀνδρός, ἐν δόμοισιν ὤν·
ἥκω δ᾽ ἕτοιμος τήνδ᾽ ἔχων σκευὴν θεοῦ·   180
δεῖ γάρ νιν ὄντα παῖδα θυγατρὸς ἐξ ἐμῆς
Διόνυσον ὃς πέφηνεν ἀνθρώποις θεὸς
ὅσον καθ᾽ ἡμᾶς δυνατὸν αὔξεσθαι μέγαν.
ποῖ δεῖ χορεύειν, ποῖ καθιστάναι πόδα
καὶ κρᾶτα σεῖσαι πολιόν; ἐξηγοῦ σύ μοι   185
γέρων γέροντι, Τειρεσία· σὺ γὰρ σοφός.
ὡς οὐ κάμοιμ᾽ ἂν οὔτε νύκτ᾽ οὔθ᾽ ἡμέραν
θύρσῳ κροτῶν γῆν· ἐπιλελήσμεθ᾽ ἡδέως
γέροντες ὄντες.

ΤΕΙΡΕΣΙΑΣ
ταῦτ᾽ ἐμοὶ πάσχεις ἄρα·
κἀγὼ γὰρ ἡβῶ κἀπιχειρήσω χοροῖς.   190

ΚΑΔΜΟΣ
οὐκοῦν ὄχοισιν εἰς ὄρος περάσομεν;

ΤΕΙΡΕΣΙΑΣ
ἀλλ᾽ οὐχ ὁμοίως ἂν ὁ θεὸς τιμὴν ἔχοι.

[Enter Tiresias, a very old blind man, dressed in clothing appropriate for the Dionysian ritual. He goes up to the palace door and knocks very aggressively]

TIRESIAS *[shouting]*

Where's the servant on the door? You in there,   [170]
tell Cadmus to get himself out of the house,
Agenor's lad, who came here from Sidon,
then put up the towers of this Theban town.[8]
Go tell him Tiresias is waiting for him.
He knows well enough why I've come for him.
I'm an old man, and he's even older,
but we've agreed make ourselves a thyrsus,
to put on fawn skins and crown our heads
with garlands of these ivy branches.

[Enter Cadmus from the palace, a very old man, also dressed in clothing appropriate for the Dionysian ritual]

CADMUS

                         My dearest friend,
I was inside the house. I heard your voice.
I recognized it — the voice of a man truly wise.
So I've come equipped with all this god stuff.   [180]
We must sing his praise, as much as we can,
for this Dionysus, well, he's my daughter's child.
Now he's revealed himself a god to men.
Where must I go and dance? Where do I get
to move my feet and shake my old gray head?
You must guide me, Tiresias, one old man
leading another, for you're the expert here.
O I'll never tire of waving this thyrsus,
day and night, striking the ground. What rapture!
Now we can forget that we're old men.

TIRESIAS

You feel the same way I do, then.
For I'm young and going to try the dancing.   [190]

CADMUS

Shall we go up the mountain in a chariot?

TIRESIAS

The god would not then get complete respect.

17

Euripides

ΚΑΔΜΟΣ
γέρων γέροντα παιδαγωγήσω σ' ἐγώ.

ΤΕΙΡΕΣΙΑΣ
ὁ θεὸς ἀμοχθὶ κεῖσε νῷν ἡγήσεται.

ΚΑΔΜΟΣ
μόνοι δὲ πόλεως Βακχίῳ χορεύσομεν;   195

ΤΕΙΡΕΣΙΑΣ
μόνοι γὰρ εὖ φρονοῦμεν, οἱ δ' ἄλλοι κακῶς.

ΚΑΔΜΟΣ
μακρὸν τὸ μέλλειν· ἀλλ' ἐμῆς ἔχου χερός.

ΤΕΙΡΕΣΙΑΣ
ἰδού, ξύναπτε καὶ ξυνωρίζου χέρα.

ΚΑΔΜΟΣ
οὐ καταφρονῶ 'γὼ τῶν θεῶν θνητὸς γεγώς.

ΤΕΙΡΕΣΙΑΣ
οὐδὲν σοφιζόμεσθα τοῖσι δαίμοσιν.   200
πατρίους παραδοχάς, ἅς θ' ὁμήλικας χρόνῳ
κεκτήμεθ', οὐδεὶς αὐτὰ καταβαλεῖ λόγος,
οὐδ' εἰ δι' ἄκρων τὸ σοφὸν ηὕρηται φρενῶν.
ἐρεῖ τις ὡς τὸ γῆρας οὐκ αἰσχύνομαι,
μέλλων χορεύειν κρᾶτα κισσώσας ἐμόν;   205
οὐ γὰρ διήρηχ' ὁ θεός, οὔτε τὸν νέον
εἰ χρὴ χορεύειν οὔτε τὸν γεραίτερον,
ἀλλ' ἐξ ἁπάντων βούλεται τιμὰς ἔχειν
κοινάς, διαριθμῶν δ' οὐδέν' αὔξεσθαι θέλει.

ΚΑΔΜΟΣ
ἐπεὶ σὺ φέγγος, Τειρεσία, τόδ' οὐχ ὁρᾷς,   210
ἐγὼ προφήτης σοι λόγων γενήσομαι.

18

CADMUS

    So I'll be your nursemaid — one old man
    will take charge of another one?

TIRESIAS

                              The god himself
    will get us to the place without our efforts.

CADMUS

    Of all the city are we the only ones
    who'll dance to honour Bacchus?

TIRESIAS

                             Yes, indeed,
    for we're the only ones whose minds are clear.
    As for the others, well, their thinking's wrong.

CADMUS

    There'll be a long wait. Take my hand.

TIRESIAS [*holding out his hand*]

    Here. Take it — make a pair of it and yours.

CADMUS

    I'm a mortal, so I don't mock the gods.

TIRESIAS

    To the gods we mortals are all ignorant.   [200]
    Those old traditions from our ancestors,
    the ones we've had as long as time itself,
    no argument will ever overthrow,
    in spite of subtleties sharp minds invent.
    Will someone say I disrespect old age,
    if I intend to dance with ivy on my head?
    Not so, for the god makes no distinctions —
    whether the dancing is for young or old.
    He wants to gather honours from us all,
    to be praised communally, without division.

CADMUS

    Since you're blind to daylight, Tiresias,   [210]
    I'll be your seer, tell you what's going on —

19

Euripides

Πενθεὺς πρὸς οἴκους ὅδε διὰ σπουδῆς περᾷ,
Ἐχίονος παῖς, ᾧ κράτος δίδωμι γῆς.
ὡς ἐπτόηται· τί ποτ᾽ ἐρεῖ νεώτερον;

ΠΕΝΘΕΥΣ

ἔκδημος ὢν μὲν τῆσδ᾽ ἐτύγχανον χθονός,   215
κλύω δὲ νεοχμὰ τήνδ᾽ ἀνὰ πτόλιν κακά,
γυναῖκας ἡμῖν δώματ᾽ ἐκλελοιπέναι
πλασταῖσι βακχείαισιν, ἐν δὲ δασκίοις
ὄρεσι θοάζειν, τὸν νεωστὶ δαίμονα
Διόνυσον, ὅστις ἔστι, τιμώσας χοροῖς·   220
πλήρεις δὲ θιάσοις ἐν μέσοισιν ἑστάναι
κρατῆρας, ἄλλην δ᾽ ἄλλοσ᾽ εἰς ἐρημίαν
πτώσσουσαν εὐναῖς ἀρσένων ὑπηρετεῖν,
πρόφασιν μὲν ὡς δὴ μαινάδας θυοσκόους,
τὴν δ᾽ Ἀφροδίτην πρόσθ᾽ ἄγειν τοῦ Βακχίου.   225
ὅσας μὲν οὖν εἴληφα, δεσμίους χέρας
σῴζουσι πανδήμοισι πρόσπολοι στέγαις·
ὅσαι δ᾽ ἄπεισιν, ἐξ ὄρους θηράσομαι,
Ἰνώ τ᾽ Ἀγαύην θ᾽, ἥ μ᾽ ἔτικτ᾽ Ἐχίονι,
Ἀκταίονός τε μητέρ᾽, Αὐτονόην λέγω.   230
καὶ σφᾶς σιδηραῖς ἁρμόσας ἐν ἄρκυσιν
παύσω κακούργου τῆσδε βακχείας τάχα.
λέγουσι δ᾽ ὡς τις εἰσελήλυθε ξένος,
γόης ἐπῳδὸς Λυδίας ἀπὸ χθονός,
ξανθοῖσι βοστρύχοισιν εὐοσμῶν κόμην,   235
οἰνῶπας ὄσσοις χάριτας Ἀφροδίτης ἔχων,
ὃς ἡμέρας τε κεὐφρόνας συγγίγνεται
τελετὰς προτείνων εὐίους νεάνισιν.
εἰ δ᾽ αὐτὸν εἴσω τῆσδε λήψομαι στέγης,
παύσω κτυποῦντα θύρσον ἀνασείοντά τε   240
κόμας, τράχηλον σώματος χωρὶς τεμών.
ἐκεῖνος εἶναί φησι Διόνυσον θεόν,

20

Pentheus, that child of Echion, the one
to whom I handed over power in this land,
he's coming here, to the house. He's in a rush.
He looks so flustered. What news will he bring?

[Enter Pentheus, with some armed attendants. At first he does not notice Cadmus and Tiresias, not until he calls attention to them]

PENTHEUS

It so happens I've been away from Thebes,
but I hear about disgusting things going on,
here in the city—women leaving home
to go to silly Bacchic rituals,
cavorting there in mountain shadows,
with dances honouring some upstart god,
this Dionysus, whoever he may be. Mixing bowls   [220]
in the middle of their meetings are filled with wine.
They creep off one by one to lonely spots
to have sex with men, claiming they're Maenads
busy worshipping. But they rank Aphrodite,
goddess of sexual desire, ahead of Bacchus.
All the ones I've caught, my servants guard
in our public prison, their hands chained up.
All those who're still away, I'll chase down,
hunt them from the mountains—that includes
Agave, who bore me to Echion, Ino,
and Autonoe, Actaeon's mother.9   [230]
Once I've clamped them all in iron fetters,
I'll quickly end this perverse nastiness,
this Bacchic celebration. People say
some stranger has arrived, some wizard,
a conjurer from the land of Lydia—
with sweet-smelling hair in golden ringlets
and Aphrodite's charms in wine-dark eyes.
He hangs around the young girls day and night,
dangling in front of them his joyful mysteries.
If I catch him in this city, I'll stop him.
He'll make no more clatter with his thyrsus,   [240]
or wave his hair around. I'll chop off his head,
slice it right from his body. This man claims
that Dionysus is a god, alleging

ἐκεῖνος ἐν μηρῷ ποτ' ἐρράφθαι Διός,

ὃς ἐκπυροῦται λαμπάσιν κεραυνίαις

σὺν μητρί, Δίους ὅτι γάμους ἐψεύσατο.   245

ταῦτ' οὐχὶ δεινῆς ἀγχόνης ἔστ' ἄξια,

ὕβρεις ὑβρίζειν, ὅστις ἔστιν ὁ ξένος;

ἀτὰρ τόδ' ἄλλο θαῦμα, τὸν τερασκόπον

ἐν ποικίλαισι νεβρίσι Τειρεσίαν ὁρῶ

πατέρα τε μητρὸς τῆς ἐμῆς—πολὺν γέλων—   250

νάρθηκι βακχεύοντ'· ἀναίνομαι, πάτερ,

τὸ γῆρας ὑμῶν εἰσορῶν νοῦν οὐκ ἔχον.

οὐκ ἀποτινάξεις κισσόν; οὐκ ἐλευθέραν

θύρσου μεθήσεις χεῖρ', ἐμῆς μητρὸς πάτερ;

σὺ ταῦτ' ἔπεισας, Τειρεσία· τόνδ' αὖ θέλεις   255

τὸν δαίμον' ἀνθρώποισιν ἐσφέρων νέον

σκοπεῖν πτερωτοὺς κἀμπύρων μισθοὺς φέρειν.

εἰ μή σε γῆρας πολιὸν ἐξερρύετο,

καθῆσ' ἂν ἐν βάκχαισι δέσμιος μέσαις,

τελετὰς πονηρὰς εἰσάγων· γυναιξὶ γὰρ   260

ὅπου βότρυος ἐν δαιτὶ γίγνεται γάνος,

οὐχ ὑγιὲς οὐδὲν ἔτι λέγω τῶν ὀργίων.

ΧΟΡΟΣ

τῆς δυσσεβείας. ὦ ξέν', οὐκ αἰδῇ θεοὺς

Κάδμον τε τὸν σπείραντα γηγενῆ στάχυν,

Ἐχίονος δ' ὢν παῖς καταισχύνεις γένος;   265

that once upon a time he was sewn up,
stitched inside Zeus' thigh—but Dionysus
was burned to death, along with Semele,
in that lightning strike, because she'd lied.
She maintained that she'd had sex with Zeus.
All this surely merits harsh punishment,
death by hanging. Whoever this stranger is,
his insolence is an insult to me.

[noticing Cadmus and Tiresias for the first time]

Well, here's something totally astounding!
I see Tiresias, our soothsayer, all dressed up
in dappled fawn skins—my mother's father, too!   [250]
This is ridiculous. To take a thyrsus
and jump around like this.

[to Cadmus]

                                        You sir,
I don't like to see such arrant foolishness
from your old age. Why not throw out that ivy?
And, grandfather, why not let that thyrsus go?

[turning to address Tiresias]

Tiresias, you're the one who's put him up to this.
You want to bring in some new god for men,
so you'll be able to inspect more birds,
and from his sacrifices make more money.
If your gray old age did not protect you,
you'd sit in chains with all the Bacchae
for such a ceremonial perversion.   [260]
Whenever women at some banquet
start to take pleasure in the gleaming wine,
I say there's nothing healthy in their worshipping.

CHORUS LEADER

That's impiety! O stranger,
have you no reverence for the gods, for Cadmus,
who sowed that crop of men born from the earth?
You're a child of Echion—do you wish
to bring your own family into disrepute?

ΤΕΙΡΕΣΙΑΣ

ὅταν λάβῃ τις τῶν λόγων ἀνὴρ σοφὸς
καλὰς ἀφορμάς, οὐ μέγ' ἔργον εὖ λέγειν·
σὺ δ' εὔτροχον μὲν γλῶσσαν ὡς φρονῶν ἔχεις,
ἐν τοῖς λόγοισι δ' οὐκ ἔνεισί σοι φρένες.
θράσει δὲ δυνατὸς καὶ λέγειν οἷός τ' ἀνὴρ   270
κακὸς πολίτης γίγνεται νοῦν οὐκ ἔχων.
οὗτος δ' ὁ δαίμων ὁ νέος, ὃν σὺ διαγελᾷς,
οὐκ ἂν δυναίμην μέγεθος ἐξειπεῖν ὅσος
καθ' Ἑλλάδ' ἔσται. δύο γάρ, ὦ νεανία,
τὰ πρῶτ' ἐν ἀνθρώποισι· Δημήτηρ θεά—   275
γῆ δ' ἐστίν, ὄνομα δ' ὁπότερον βούλῃ κάλει·
αὕτη μὲν ἐν ξηροῖσιν ἐκτρέφει βροτούς·
ὃς δ' ἦλθ' ἔπειτ', ἀντίπαλον ὁ Σεμέλης γόνος
βότρυος ὑγρὸν πῶμ' ηὗρε κεἰσηνέγκατο
θνητοῖς, ὃ παύει τοὺς ταλαιπώρους βροτοὺς   280
λύπης, ὅταν πλησθῶσιν ἀμπέλου ῥοῆς,
ὕπνον τε λήθην τῶν καθ' ἡμέραν κακῶν
δίδωσιν, οὐδ' ἔστ' ἄλλο φάρμακον πόνων.
οὗτος θεοῖσι σπένδεται θεὸς γεγώς,
ὥστε διὰ τοῦτον τἀγάθ' ἀνθρώπους ἔχειν.   285
καὶ καταγελᾷς νιν, ὡς ἐνερράφη Διὸς
μηρῷ; διδάξω σ' ὡς καλῶς ἔχει τόδε.
ἐπεί νιν ἥρπασ' ἐκ πυρὸς κεραυνίου
Ζεύς, ἐς δ' Ὄλυμπον βρέφος ἀνήγαγεν θεόν,
Ἥρα νιν ἤθελ' ἐκβαλεῖν ἀπ' οὐρανοῦ·   290
Ζεὺς δ' ἀντεμηχανήσαθ' οἷα δὴ θεός.
ῥήξας μέρος τι τοῦ χθόν' ἐγκυκλουμένου
αἰθέρος, ἔθηκε τόνδ' ὅμηρον ἐκδιδούς,
Διόνυσον Ἥρας νεικέων· χρόνῳ δέ νιν

TIRESIAS

    When a man of wisdom has good occasion
    to speak out, and takes the opportunity,
    it's not that hard to give an excellent speech.
    You've got a quick tongue and seem intelligent,
    but your words don't make any sense at all.
    A fluent orator whose power comes   [270]
    from self-assurance and from nothing else
    makes a bad citizen, for he lacks sense.
    This man, this new god, whom you ridicule—
    it's impossible for me to tell you
    just how great he'll be in all of Greece.
    Young man, among human beings two things
    stand out preeminent, of highest rank.
    Goddess Demeter is one—she's the earth
    (though you can call her any name you wish),
    and she feeds mortal people cereal grains.
    The other one came later, born of Semele—
    he brought with him liquor from the grape,
    something to match the bread from Demeter.
    He introduced it among mortal men.
    When they can drink up what streams off the vine,
    unhappy mortals are released from pain.   [280]
    It grants them sleep, allows them to forget
    their daily troubles. Apart from wine,
    there is no cure for human hardship.
    He, being a god, is poured out to the gods,
    so human beings receive fine benefits
    as gifts from him. And yet you mock him. Why?
    Because he was sewn into Zeus thigh?
    Well, I'll show you how this all makes sense.
    When Zeus grabbed him from the lightning flame,
    he brought him to Olympus as a god.
    But Hera wished to throw him out of heaven.   [290]
    So Zeus, in a manner worthy of a god,
    came up with a cunning counter plan.
    From the sky which flows around the earth,
    Zeus broke off a piece, shaped it like Dionysus,
    then gave that to Hera, as a hostage.
    The real child he sent to nymphs to raise,
    thus saving him from Hera's jealousy.
    Over time people mixed up "sky" and "thigh,"

βροτοὶ ῥαφῆναί φασιν ἐν μηρῷ Διός, 295
ὄνομα μεταστήσαντες, ὅτι θεᾷ θεὸς
Ἥρᾳ ποθ' ὡμήρευσε, συνθέντες λόγον.
μάντις δ' ὁ δαίμων ὅδε· τὸ γὰρ βακχεύσιμον
καὶ τὸ μανιῶδες μαντικὴν πολλὴν ἔχει·
ὅταν γὰρ ὁ θεὸς ἐς τὸ σῶμ' ἔλθῃ πολύς, 300
λέγειν τὸ μέλλον τοὺς μεμηνότας ποιεῖ.
Ἄρεώς τε μοῖραν μεταλαβὼν ἔχει τινά·
στρατὸν γὰρ ἐν ὅπλοις ὄντα κἀπὶ τάξεσιν
φόβος διεπτόησε πρὶν λόγχης θιγεῖν.
μανία δὲ καὶ τοῦτ' ἐστὶ Διονύσου πάρα. 305
ἔτ' αὐτὸν ὄψῃ κἀπὶ Δελφίσιν πέτραις
πηδῶντα σὺν πεύκαισι δικόρυφον πλάκα,
πάλλοντα καὶ σείοντα βακχεῖον κλάδον,
μέγαν τ' ἀν' Ἑλλάδα. ἀλλ' ἐμοί, Πενθεῦ, πιθοῦ·
μὴ τὸ κράτος αὔχει δύναμιν ἀνθρώποις ἔχειν, 310
μηδ', ἢν δοκῇς μέν, ἡ δὲ δόξα σου νοσῇ,
φρονεῖν δόκει τι· τὸν θεὸν δ' ἐς γῆν δέχου
καὶ σπένδε καὶ βάκχευε καὶ στέφου κάρα.
οὐχ ὁ Διόνυσος σωφρονεῖν ἀναγκάσει
γυναῖκας ἐς τὴν Κύπριν, ἀλλ' ἐν τῇ φύσει 315
τὸ σωφρονεῖν ἔνεστιν εἰς τὰ πάντ' ἀεί
τοῦτο σκοπεῖν χρή· καὶ γὰρ ἐν βακχεύμασιν
οὖσ' ἥ γε σώφρων οὐ διαφθαρήσεται.
ὁρᾷς, σὺ χαίρεις, ὅταν ἐφεστῶσιν πύλαις
πολλοί, τὸ Πενθέως δ' ὄνομα μεγαλύνῃ πόλις· 320
κἀκεῖνος, οἶμαι, τέρπεται τιμώμενος.
ἐγὼ μὲν οὖν καὶ Κάδμος, ὃν σὺ διαγελᾷς,
κισσῷ τ' ἐρεψόμεσθα καὶ χορεύσομεν,
πολιὰ ξυνωρίς, ἀλλ' ὅμως χορευτέον,
κοὐ θεομαχήσω σῶν λόγων πεισθεὶς ὕπο. 325

saying he'd come from Zeus's thigh, changing words,
because he, a god, had once been hostage
to goddess Hera. So they made up the tale.
This god's a prophet, too, for in his rites—
the Bacchic celebrations and the madness—
a huge prophetic power is unleashed.
When the god fully enters human bodies,   [300]
he makes those possessed by frenzy prophets.
They speak of what will come in future days
He also shares the work of war god Ares.
For there are times an army all drawn up,
its weapons ready, can shake with terror,
before any man has set hand to his spear.
Such madness comes from Dionysus.
Some day you'll see him on those rocks at Delphi,
leaping with torches on the higher slopes,
way up there between two mountain peaks,
waving and shaking his Bacchic wand,
a great power in Greece. Trust me, Pentheus.
Don't be too confident a sovereign's force
controls men. If something seems right to you,   [310]
but your mind's diseased, don't think that's wisdom.
So welcome this god into your country.
Pour libations to him, then celebrate
these Bacchic rites with garlands on your head.
On women, where Aphrodite is concerned,
Dionysus will not enforce restraint—
such modesty you must seek in nature,
where it already dwells. For any woman
whose character is chaste won't be defiled
by Bacchic revelry. Don't you see that?
When there are many people at your gates,
you're happy. The city shouts your praise.
It celebrates the name of Pentheus.   [320]
The god, too, I think, derives great pleasure
from being honoured. And so Cadmus,
whom you mock, and I will crown our heads
with ivy and will join the ritual,
an old gray team, but still we have to dance.
Your words will not turn me against the god,

27

Euripides

μαίνῃ γὰρ ὡς ἄλγιστα, κοὔτε φαρμάκοις
ἄκη λάβοις ἂν οὔτ᾽ ἄνευ τούτων νοσεῖς.

ΧΟΡΟΣ

ὦ πρέσβυ, Φοῖβόν τ᾽ οὐ καταισχύνεις λόγοις,
τιμῶν τε Βρόμιον σωφρονεῖς, μέγαν θεόν.

ΚΑΔΜΟΣ

ὦ παῖ, καλῶς σοι Τειρεσίας παρῄνεσεν.   330
οἴκει μεθ᾽ ἡμῶν, μὴ θύραζε τῶν νόμων.
νῦν γὰρ πέτῃ τε καὶ φρονῶν οὐδὲν φρονεῖς.
κεἰ μὴ γὰρ ἔστιν ὁ θεὸς οὗτος, ὡς σὺ φής,
παρὰ σοὶ λεγέσθω· καὶ καταψεύδου καλῶς
ὡς ἔστι, Σεμέλη θ᾽ ἵνα δοκῇ θεὸν τεκεῖν,   335
ἡμῖν τε τιμὴ παντὶ τῷ γένει προσῇ.
ὁρᾷς τὸν Ἀκτέωνος ἄθλιον μόρον,
ὃν ὠμόσιτοι σκύλακες ἃς ἐθρέψατο
διεσπάσαντο, κρείσσον᾽ ἐν κυναγίαις
Ἀρτέμιδος εἶναι κομπάσαντ᾽, ἐν ὀργάσιν.   340
ὃ μὴ πάθῃς σύ· δεῦρό σου στέψω κάρα
κισσῷ· μεθ᾽ ἡμῶν τῷ θεῷ τιμὴν δίδου.

ΠΕΝΘΕΥΣ

οὐ μὴ προσοίσεις χεῖρα, βακχεύσεις δ᾽ ἰών,
μηδ᾽ ἐξομόρξῃ μωρίαν τὴν σὴν ἐμοί;
τῆς σῆς δ᾽ ἀνοίας τόνδε τὸν διδάσκαλον   345
δίκην μέτειμι. στειχέτω τις ὡς τάχος,
ἐλθὼν δὲ θάκους τοῦδ᾽ ἵν᾽ οἰωνοσκοπεῖ
μοχλοῖς τριαίνου κἀνάτρεψον ἔμπαλιν,
ἄνω κάτω τὰ πάντα συγχέας ὁμοῦ,
καὶ στέμματ᾽ ἀνέμοις καὶ θυέλλαισιν μέθες.   350
μάλιστα γάρ νιν δήξομαι δράσας τάδε.

28

for you are mad — under a cruel delusion.
No drug can heal that ailment — in fact,
some drug has caused it.

CHORUS LEADER

Old man,
you've not disgraced Apollo with your words,
and by honouring this Dionysus,
a great god, you show your moderation.

CADMUS

My child, Tiresias has given you   [330]
some good advice. You should live among us,
not outside traditions. At this point,
you're flying around — thinking, but not clearly.
For if, as you claim, this man is not a god,
why not call him one? Why not tell a lie,
a really good one? Then it will seem
that some god has been born to Semele.
We — and all our family — will win honour.
Remember the dismal fate of Actaeon —
torn to pieces in some mountain forest
by blood-thirsty dogs he'd raised himself.
He'd boasted he was better in the hunt   [340]
than Artemis. Don't suffer the same fate.
Come here. Let me crown your head with ivy.
Join us in giving honour to this god.

PENTHEUS

Keep your hands off me! Be off with you —
go to these Bacchic rituals of yours.
But don't infect me with your madness.
As for the one who in this foolishness
has been your teacher, I'll bring him to justice.

[to his attendants]

One of you, go quickly to where this man,
Tiresias, has that seat of his, the place
where he inspects his birds. Take some levers,
knock it down. Demolish it completely.
Turn the whole place upside down — all of it.
Let his holy ribbons fly off in the winds.   [350]
That way I'll really do him damage.

29

Euripides

οἳ δ' ἀνὰ πόλιν στείχοντες ἐξιχνεύσατε
τὸν θηλύμορφον ξένον, ὃς ἐσφέρει νόσον
καινὴν γυναιξὶ καὶ λέχη λυμαίνεται.
κἄνπερ λάβητε, δέσμιον πορεύσατε   355
δεῦρ' αὐτόν, ὡς ἂν λευσίμου δίκης τυχὼν
θάνῃ, πικρὰν βάκχευσιν ἐν Θήβαις ἰδών.

ΤΕΙΡΕΣΙΑΣ
ὦ σχέτλι', ὡς οὐκ οἶσθα ποῦ ποτ' εἶ λόγων.
μέμηνας ἤδη· καὶ πρὶν ἐξέστης φρενῶν.
στείχωμεν ἡμεῖς, Κάδμε, κἀξαιτώμεθα   360
ὑπέρ τε τούτου καίπερ ὄντος ἀγρίου
ὑπέρ τε πόλεως τὸν θεὸν μηδὲν νέον
δρᾶν. ἀλλ' ἕπου μοι κισσίνου βάκτρου μέτα,
πειρῶ δ' ἀνορθοῦν σῶμ' ἐμόν, κἀγὼ τὸ σόν·
γέροντε δ' αἰσχρὸν δύο πεσεῖν· ἴτω δ' ὅμως,   365
τῷ Βακχίῳ γὰρ τῷ Διὸς δουλευτέον.
Πενθεὺς δ' ὅπως μὴ πένθος εἰσοίσει δόμοις
τοῖς σοῖσι, Κάδμε· μαντικῇ μὲν οὐ λέγω,
τοῖς πράγμασιν δέ· μῶρα γὰρ μῶρος λέγει.

ΧΟΡΟΣ
Ὁσία πότνα θεῶν,   370
Ὁσία δ' ἃ κατὰ γᾶν
χρυσέαν πτέρυγα φέρεις,
τάδε Πενθέως ἀίεις;
ἀίεις οὐχ ὁσίαν
ὕβριν ἐς τὸν Βρόμιον, τὸν   375
Σεμέλας, τὸν παρὰ καλλι-
στεφάνοις εὐφροσύναις δαίμονα πρῶτον μακάρων; ὃς τάδ' ἔχει,
θιασεύειν τε χοροῖς
μετά τ' αὐλοῦ γελάσαι   380

30

You others—go to the city, scour it
to capture this effeminate stranger,
who corrupts our women with a new disease,
and thus infects our beds. If you get him,
tie him up and bring him here for judgment,
a death by stoning. That way he'll see
his rites in Thebes come to a bitter end.

[Exit Pentheus into the palace]

TIRESIAS

You unhappy man, you've no idea
just what it is you're saying. You've gone mad!
Even before now you weren't in your right mind.
Let's be off, Cadmus. We'll pray to the god   [360]
on Pentheus' behalf, though he's a savage,
and for the city, too, so he won't harm it.
Come with me—bring the ivy-covered staff.
See if you can help support my body.
I'll do the same for you. It would be shameful
if two old men collapsed. No matter—
for we must serve Bacchus, son of Zeus.
But you, Cadmus, you should be more careful,
or Pentheus will bring trouble in your home.
I'm not saying this as a prophecy,
but on the basis of what's going on.
A man who's mad tends to utter madness.

[Exit Tiresias and Cadmus together on their way to the mountains]

CHORUS

Holiness, queen of the gods,   [370]
Holiness, sweeping over earth
on wings of gold,
do you hear what Pentheus says?
Do you hear the profanities he utters,
the insults against Bromius,
child of Semele, chief god
among all blessed gods,
for those who wear their lovely garlands
in a spirit of harmonious joy?
This is his special office,
to lead men together in the dance,
to make them laugh as the flute plays,   [380]

ἀποπαῦσαί τε μερίμνας,
ὁπόταν βότρυος ἔλθῃ
γάνος ἐν δαιτὶ θεῶν, κισ-
σοφόροις δ' ἐν θαλίαις ἀν-
δράσι κρατὴρ ὕπνον ἀμ-   385
φιβάλλῃ.

ἀχαλίνων στομάτων
ἀνόμου τ' ἀφροσύνας
τὸ τέλος δυστυχία·
ὁ δὲ τᾶς ἡσυχίας
βίοτος καὶ τὸ φρονεῖν   390
ἀσάλευτόν τε μένει καὶ
συνέχει δώματα· πόρσω
γὰρ ὅμως αἰθέρα ναίον-
τες ὁρῶσιν τὰ βροτῶν οὐρανίδαι.
τὸ σοφὸν δ' οὐ σοφία   395
τό τε μὴ θνητὰ φρονεῖν.
βραχὺς αἰών· ἐπὶ τούτῳ
δέ τις ἂν μεγάλα διώκων
τὰ παρόντ' οὐχὶ φέροι. μαι-
νομένων οἵδε τρόποι καὶ   400
κακοβούλων παρ' ἔμοι-
γε φωτῶν.

ἱκοίμαν ποτὶ Κύπρον,
νᾶσον τᾶς Ἀφροδίτας,
ἵν' οἱ θελξίφρονες νέμον-
ται θνατοῖσιν Ἔρωτες,   405
Πάφον θ' ἂν ἑκατόστομοι
βαρβάρου ποταμοῦ ῥοαὶ
καρπίζουσιν ἄνομβροι.
οὗ δ' ἁ καλλιστευομένα
Πιερία μούσειος ἕδρα,   410
σεμνὰ κλιτὺς Ὀλύμπου,
ἐκεῖσ' ἄγε με, Βρόμιε Βρόμιε,
πρόβακχ' εὔιε δαῖμον.

to bring all sorrows to an end,
at the god's sacrificial feast,
when the gleaming liquid grapes arrive,
when the wine bowl casts its sleep
on ivy-covered feasting men.

Unbridled tongues and lawless folly
come to an end only in disaster.
A peaceful life of wisdom   [390]
maintains tranquillity.
It keeps the home united.
Though gods live in the sky,
from far away in heaven
they gaze upon the deeds of men.
But being clever isn't wisdom.
And thinking deeply about things
isn't suitable for mortal men.
Our life is brief—that's why
the man who chases greatness
fails to grasp what's near at hand.
That's what madmen do,   [400]
men who've lost their wits.
That's what I believe.

Would I might go to Cyprus,
island of Aphrodite,
where the Erotes,
bewitching goddesses of love,
soothe the hearts of humankind,
or to Paphos, rich and fertile,
not with rain, but with the waters
of a hundred flowing mouths
of a strange and foreign river.
O Bromius, Bromius,
inspired god who leads the Bacchae,
lead me away to lovely Peira,   [410]
where Muses dwell,
or to Olympus' sacred slopes,

33

ἐκεῖ Χάριτες,
ἐκεῖ δὲ Πόθος· ἐκεῖ δὲ βάκ-   415
χαις θέμις ὀργιάζειν.
ὁ δαίμων ὁ Διὸς παῖς
χαίρει μὲν θαλίαισιν,
φιλεῖ δ' ὀλβοδότειραν Εἰ-
ρήναν, κουροτρόφον θεάν.   420
ἴσαν δ' ἔς τε τὸν ὄλβιον
τόν τε χείρονα δῶκ' ἔχειν
οἴνου τέρψιν ἄλυπον·
μισεῖ δ' ᾧ μὴ ταῦτα μέλει,
κατὰ φάος νύκτας τε φίλας   425
εὐαίωνα διαζῆν,
σοφὰν δ' ἀπέχειν πραπίδα φρένα τε
περισσῶν παρὰ φωτῶν·
τὸ πλῆθος ὅ τι   430
τὸ φαυλότερον ἐνόμισε χρῆ-
ταί τε, τόδ' ἂν δεχοίμαν.

ΘΕΡΑΠΩΝ

Πενθεῦ, πάρεσμεν τήνδ' ἄγραν ἠγρευκότες
ἐφ' ἣν ἔπεμψας, οὐδ' ἄκρανθ' ὡρμήσαμεν.   435
ὁ θὴρ δ' ὅδ' ἡμῖν πρᾶος οὐδ' ὑπέσπασεν
φυγῇ πόδ', ἀλλ' ἔδωκεν οὐκ ἄκων χέρας
οὐδ' ὠχρός, οὐδ' ἤλλαξεν οἰνωπὸν γένυν,
γελῶν δὲ καὶ δεῖν κἀπάγειν ἐφίετο
ἔμενέ τε, τοὐμὸν εὐτρεπὲς ποιούμενος.   440
κἀγὼ δι' αἰδοῦς εἶπον· Ὦ ξέν', οὐχ ἑκὼν
ἄγω σε, Πενθέως δ' ὅς μ' ἔπεμψ' ἐπιστολαῖς.
ἃς δ' αὖ σὺ βάκχας εἶρξας, ἃς συνήρπασας
κἄδησας ἐν δεσμοῖσι πανδήμου στέγης,
φροῦδαί γ' ἐκεῖναι λελυμέναι πρὸς ὀργάδας   445
σκιρτῶσι Βρόμιον ἀνακαλούμεναι θεόν·

34

where Graces live, Desire, too,
where it's lawful and appropriate
to celebrate our rites with Bacchus.
This god, son of Zeus,
rejoices in our banquets.
He adores the goddess Peace,
and she brings riches with her   [420]
and nourishes the young.
The god gives his wine equally,
sharing with rich and poor alike.
It takes away all sorrow.
But he hates the man who doesn't care
to live his life in happiness,
by day and through the friendly nights.
From those who deny such common things
he removes intelligence,
their knowledge of true wisdom.
So I take this as my rule—
follow what common people think—   [430]
do what most men do.

[Enter a group of soldiers, bringing Dionysus with his arms tied up. Pentheus enters from the palace]

SOLDIER

Pentheus, we're here because we've caught the prey
you sent us out to catch. Yes, our attempts
have proved successful. The beast you see here
was tame with us. He didn't try to run.
No, he surrendered willingly enough,
without turning pale or changing colour
on those wine dark cheeks. He even laughed at us,
inviting us to tie him up and lead him off.   [440]
He stood still, making it easier for me
to take him in. It was awkward, so I said,
"Stranger, I don't want to lead you off,
but I'm under orders here from Pentheus,
who sent me." And there's something else—
those Bacchic women you locked up, the ones
you took in chains into the public prison—
they've all escaped. They're gone—playing around
in some meadow, calling out to Bromius,

35

Euripides

αὐτόματα δ' αὐταῖς δεσμὰ διελύθη ποδῶν
κλῇδές τ' ἀνῆκαν θύρετρ' ἄνευ θνητῆς χερός.
πολλῶν δ' ὅδ' ἀνὴρ θαυμάτων ἥκει πλέως
ἐς τάσδε Θήβας. σοὶ δὲ τἄλλα χρὴ μέλειν.   450

ΠΕΝΘΕΥΣ
    μέθεσθε χειρῶν τοῦδ'· ἐν ἄρκυσιν γὰρ ὢν
    οὐκ ἔστιν οὕτως ὠκὺς ὥστε μ' ἐκφυγεῖν.

    ἀτὰρ τὸ μὲν σῶμ' οὐκ ἄμορφος εἶ, ξένε,
    ὡς ἐς γυναῖκας, ἐφ' ὅπερ ἐς Θήβας πάρει·
    πλόκαμός τε γάρ σου ταναός, οὐ πάλης ὕπο,   455
    γένυν παρ' αὐτὴν κεχυμένος, πόθου πλέως·
    λευκὴν δὲ χροιὰν ἐκ παρασκευῆς ἔχεις,
    οὐχ ἡλίου βολαῖσιν, ἀλλ' ὑπὸ σκιᾶς,
    τὴν Ἀφροδίτην καλλονῇ θηρώμενος.
    πρῶτον μὲν οὖν μοι λέξον ὅστις εἶ γένος.   460

ΔΙΟΝΥΣΟΣ
    οὐ κόμπος οὐδείς· ῥᾴδιον δ' εἰπεῖν τόδε.
    τὸν ἀνθεμώδη Τμῶλον οἶσθά που κλύων.

ΠΕΝΘΕΥΣ
    οἶδ', ὃς τὸ Σάρδεων ἄστυ περιβάλλει κύκλῳ.

ΔΙΟΝΥΣΟΣ
    ἐντεῦθέν εἰμι, Λυδία δέ μοι πατρίς.

ΠΕΝΘΕΥΣ
    πόθεν δὲ τελετὰς τάσδ' ἄγεις ἐς Ἑλλάδα;   465

ΔΙΟΝΥΣΟΣ
    Διόνυσος ἡμᾶς εἰσέβησ', ὁ τοῦ Διός.

ΠΕΝΘΕΥΣ
    Ζεὺς δ' ἔστ' ἐκεῖ τις, ὃς νέους τίκτει θεούς;

ΔΙΟΝΥΣΟΣ
    οὔκ, ἀλλ' ὁ Σεμέλην ἐνθάδε ζεύξας γάμοις.

36

summoning their god. Chains fell off their feet,
just dropping on their own. Keys opened doors
not turned by human hands. This man here
has come to Thebes full of amazing tricks.
But now the rest of this affair is up to you.   [450]

[Soldier hands chained Dionysus over to Pentheus]

PENTHEUS *[moving up close to Dionysus, inspecting him carefully]*
Untie his hands. I've got him in my nets.
He's not fast enough to get away from me.

[Soldiers remove the chains from Dionysus' hands. Pentheus moves in closer]

Well, stranger, I see this body of yours
is not unsuitable for women's pleasure —
that's why you've come to Thebes. As for your hair,
it's long, which suggests that you're no wrestler.
It flows across your cheeks   That's most seductive.
You've a white skin, too. You've looked after it,
avoiding the sun's rays by staying in the shade,
while with your beauty you chase Aphrodite.
But first tell me something of your family.   [460]

DIONYSUS
That's easy enough, though I'm not boasting.
You've heard of Tmolus, where flowers grow.

PENTHEUS
I know it. It's around the town of Sardis.

DIONYSUS
I'm from there. My home land is Lydia.

PENTHEUS
Why do you bring these rituals to Greece?

DIONYSUS
Dionysus sent me — the son of Zeus.

PENTHEUS
Is there some Zeus there who creates new gods?

DIONYSUS
No. It's the same Zeus who wed Semele right here.

ΠΕΝΘΕΥΣ

πότερα δὲ νύκτωρ σ᾽ ἢ κατ᾽ ὄμμ᾽ ἠνάγκασεν;

ΔΙΟΝΥΣΟΣ

ὁρῶν ὁρῶντα, καὶ δίδωσιν ὄργια. 470

ΠΕΝΘΕΥΣ

τὰ δ᾽ ὄργι᾽ ἐστὶ τίν᾽ ἰδέαν ἔχοντά σοι;

ΔΙΟΝΥΣΟΣ

ἄρρητ᾽ ἀβακχεύτοισιν εἰδέναι βροτῶν.

ΠΕΝΘΕΥΣ

ἔχει δ᾽ ὄνησιν τοῖσι θύουσιν τίνα;

ΔΙΟΝΥΣΟΣ

οὐ θέμις ἀκοῦσαί σ᾽, ἔστι δ᾽ ἄξι᾽ εἰδέναι.

ΠΕΝΘΕΥΣ

εὖ τοῦτ᾽ ἐκιβδήλευσας, ἵν᾽ ἀκοῦσαι θέλω. 475

ΔΙΟΝΥΣΟΣ

ἀσέβειαν ἀσκοῦντ᾽ ὄργι᾽ ἐχθαίρει θεοῦ.

ΠΕΝΘΕΥΣ

τὸν θεὸν ὁρᾶν γὰρ φῂς σαφῶς, ποῖός τις ἦν;

ΔΙΟΝΥΣΟΣ

ὁποῖος ἤθελ᾽· οὐκ ἐγὼ ᾽τασσον τόδε.

ΠΕΝΘΕΥΣ

τοῦτ᾽ αὖ παρωχέτευσας εὖ κοὐδὲν λέγων.

ΔΙΟΝΥΣΟΣ

δόξει τις ἀμαθεῖ σοφὰ λέγων οὐκ εὖ φρονεῖν. 480

PENTHEUS

    Did this Zeus overpower you at night,
    in your dreams? Or were your eyes wide open?

DIONYSUS

    I saw him—he saw me. He gave me   [470]
    the sacred rituals.

PENTHEUS

                    Tell me what they're like,
    those rituals of yours.

DIONYSUS

                    That information
    cannot be passed on to men like you,
    those uninitiated in the rites of Bacchus.

PENTHEUS

    Do they benefit those who sacrifice?

DIONYSUS

    They're worth knowing, but you're not allowed to hear.

PENTHEUS

    You've avoided that question skillfully,
    making me want to hear an answer.

DIONYSUS

    The rituals are no friend of any man
    who's hostile to the gods.

PENTHEUS

                    This god of yours,
    since you saw him clearly, what's he like?

DIONYSUS

    He was what he wished to be, not made to order.

PENTHEUS

    Again you fluently evade my question,
    saying nothing whatsoever.

DIONYSUS

                Yes, but then
    a man can seem totally ignorant
    when speaking to a fool.   [480]

ΠΕΝΘΕΥΣ
    ἦλθες δὲ πρῶτα δεῦρ' ἄγων τὸν δαίμονα;

ΔΙΟΝΥΣΟΣ
    πᾶς ἀναχορεύει βαρβάρων τάδ' ὄργια.

ΠΕΝΘΕΥΣ
    φρονοῦσι γὰρ κάκιον Ἑλλήνων πολύ.

ΔΙΟΝΥΣΟΣ
    τάδ' εὖ γε μᾶλλον· οἱ νόμοι δὲ διάφοροι.

ΠΕΝΘΕΥΣ
    τὰ δ' ἱερὰ νύκτωρ ἢ μεθ' ἡμέραν τελεῖς;   485

ΔΙΟΝΥΣΟΣ
    νύκτωρ τὰ πολλά· σεμνότητ' ἔχει σκότος.

ΠΕΝΘΕΥΣ
    τοῦτ' ἐς γυναῖκας δόλιόν ἐστι καὶ σαθρόν.

ΔΙΟΝΥΣΟΣ
    κἀν ἡμέρᾳ τό γ' αἰσχρὸν ἐξεύροι τις ἄν.

ΠΕΝΘΕΥΣ
    δίκην σε δοῦναι δεῖ σοφισμάτων κακῶν.

ΔΙΟΝΥΣΟΣ
    σὲ δ' ἀμαθίας γε κἀσεβοῦντ' ἐς τὸν θεόν.   490

ΠΕΝΘΕΥΣ
    ὡς θρασὺς ὁ βάκχος κοὐκ ἀγύμναστος λόγων.

ΔΙΟΝΥΣΟΣ
    εἴφ' ὅ τι παθεῖν δεῖ· τί με τὸ δεινὸν ἐργάσῃ;

ΠΕΝΘΕΥΣ
    πρῶτον μὲν ἁβρὸν βόστρυχον τεμῶ σέθεν.

ΔΙΟΝΥΣΟΣ
    ἱερὸς ὁ πλόκαμος· τῷ θεῷ δ' αὐτὸν τρέφω.

PENTHEUS

                                     Is Thebes
the first place you've come to with your god?

DIONYSUS

All the barbarians are dancing in these rites.[10]

PENTHEUS

I'm not surprised. They're stupider than Greeks.

DIONYSUS

In this they are much wiser. But their laws
are very different, too.

PENTHEUS

                       When you dance these rites,
is it at night or during daylight?

DIONYSUS

Mainly at night. Shadows confer solemnity.

PENTHEUS

And deceive the women. It's all corrupt!

DIONYSUS

One can do shameful things in daylight, too.

PENTHEUS

You must be punished for these evil games.

DIONYSUS

You, too — for foolishness, impiety
towards the god.   [490]

PENTHEUS

                    How brash this Bacchant is!
How well prepared in using language!

DIONYSUS

What punishment am I to suffer?
What harsh penalties will you inflict?

PENTHEUS

First, I'll cut off this delicate hair of yours.

DIONYSUS

My hair is sacred. I grow it for the god.

41

ΠΕΝΘΕΥΣ

ἔπειτα θύρσον τόνδε παράδος ἐκ χεροῖν.   495

ΔΙΟΝΥΣΟΣ

αὐτός μ' ἀφαιροῦ· τόνδε Διονύσου φορῶ.

ΠΕΝΘΕΥΣ

εἰρκταῖσί τ' ἔνδον σῶμα σὸν φυλάξομεν.

ΔΙΟΝΥΣΟΣ

λύσει μ' ὁ δαίμων αὐτός, ὅταν ἐγὼ θέλω.

ΠΕΝΘΕΥΣ

ὅταν γε καλέσῃς αὐτὸν ἐν βάκχαις σταθείς.

ΔΙΟΝΥΣΟΣ

καὶ νῦν ἃ πάσχω πλησίον παρὼν ὁρᾷ.   500

ΠΕΝΘΕΥΣ

καὶ ποῦ 'στιν; οὐ γὰρ φανερὸς ὄμμασίν γ' ἐμοῖς.

ΔΙΟΝΥΣΟΣ

παρ' ἐμοί· σὺ δ' ἀσεβὴς αὐτὸς ὢν οὐκ εἰσορᾷς.

ΠΕΝΘΕΥΣ

λάζυσθε· καταφρονεῖ με καὶ Θήβας ὅδε.

ΔΙΟΝΥΣΟΣ

αὐδῶ με μὴ δεῖν σωφρονῶν οὐ σώφροσιν.

ΠΕΝΘΕΥΣ

ἐγὼ δὲ δεῖν γε, κυριώτερος σέθεν.   505

ΔΙΟΝΥΣΟΣ

οὐκ οἶσθ' ὅ τι ζῇς, οὐδ' ὃ δρᾷς, οὐδ' ὅστις εἶ.

ΠΕΝΘΕΥΣ

Πενθεύς, Ἀγαύης παῖς, πατρὸς δ' Ἐχίονος.

PENTHEUS

> And give me that thyrsus in your hand.

DIONYSUS

> This wand I carry is the god's, not mine.
> You'll have to seize it from me for yourself.

PENTHEUS

> We'll lock your body up inside, in prison.

DIONYSUS

> The god will personally set me free,
> whenever I so choose.

PENTHEUS

> That only works
> if you call him while among the Bacchae.

DIONYSUS

> He sees my suffering now — and from near by.   [500]

PENTHEUS

> Where is he then? My eyes don't see him.

DIONYSUS

> He's where I am. You can't see him,
> because you don't believe.

PENTHEUS *[to his attendants]*

> Seize him!
> He's insulting Thebes and me.

DIONYSUS

> I warn you — you shouldn't tie me up.
> I've got my wits about me. You've lost yours.

PENTHEUS

> But I'm more powerful than you,
> so I'll have you put in chains.

DIONYSUS

> You're quite ignorant
> of why you live, what you do, and who you are.

PENTHEUS

> I am Pentheus, son of Agave and Echion.

Euripides

ΔΙΟΝΥΣΟΣ

ἐνδυστυχῆσαι τοὔνομ' ἐπιτήδειος εἶ.

ΠΕΝΘΕΥΣ

χώρει· καθείρξατ' αὐτὸν ἱππικαῖς πέλας
φάτναισιν, ὡς ἂν σκότιον εἰσορᾷ κνέφας.   510
ἐκεῖ χόρευε· τάσδε δ' ἃς ἄγων πάρει
κακῶν συνεργοὺς ἢ διεμπολήσομεν
ἢ χεῖρα δούπου τοῦδε καὶ βύρσης κτύπου
παύσας, ἐφ' ἱστοῖς δμωίδας κεκτήσομαι.

ΔΙΟΝΥΣΟΣ

στείχοιμ' ἄν· ὅ τι γὰρ μὴ χρεών, οὔτοι χρεὼν   515
παθεῖν. ἀτάρ τοι τῶνδ' ἄποιν' ὑβρισμάτων
μέτεισι Διόνυσός σ', ὃν οὐκ εἶναι λέγεις·
ἡμᾶς γὰρ ἀδικῶν κεῖνον εἰς δεσμοὺς ἄγεις.

ΧΟΡΟΣ

Ἀχελῴου θύγατερ,
πότνι' εὐπάρθενε Δίρκα,   520
σὺ γὰρ ἐν σαῖς ποτε παγαῖς
τὸ Διὸς βρέφος ἔλαβες,
ὅτε μηρῷ πυρὸς ἐξ ἀ-
θανάτου Ζεὺς ὁ τεκὼν ἥρ-
πασέ νιν, τάδ' ἀναβοάσας·   525
Ἴθι, Διθύραμβ', ἐμὰν ἄρ-
σενα τάνδε βᾶθι νηδύν·
ἀναφαίνω σε τόδ', ὦ Βάκ-
χιε, Θήβαις ὀνομάζειν.
σὺ δέ μ', ὦ μάκαιρα Δίρκα,   530
στεφανηφόρους ἀπωθῇ
θιάσους ἔχουσαν ἐν σοί.

44

DIONYSUS

A suitable name. It suggests misfortune.

PENTHEUS *[to his soldiers]*

Go now.
Lock him up—in the adjoining stables.
That way he'll see nothing but the darkness   [510]
There you can dance. As for all those women,
those partners in crime you brought along with you,
we'll sell them off or keep them here as slaves,
working our looms, once we've stopped their hands
beating those drum skins, making all that noise.

[Exit Pentheus into the palace, leaving Dionysus with the soldiers]

DIONYSUS

I'll go, then. For I won't have to suffer
what won't occur. But you can be sure of this—
Dionysus, whom you claim does not exist,
will go after you for retribution
after all your insolence. He's the one
you put in chains when you treat me unjustly.

[The soldiers lead Dionysus away to an area beside the palace]

CHORUS

O Sacred Dirce, blessed maiden,
daughter of Achelous,   [520]
your streams once received
the new-born child of Zeus,
when his father snatched him
from those immortal fires,
then hid him in his thigh,
crying out these words,
"Go, Dithyrambus,
enter my male womb.
I'll make you known as Bacchus
to all those in Thebes,
who'll invoke you with that name."
But you, O sacred Dirce,   [530]
why do you resist me,
my garland-bearing company,
along your river banks?

45

τί μ' ἀναίνῃ; τί με φεύγεις;
ἔτι ναὶ τὰν βοτρυώδη
Διονύσου χάριν οἴνας,   535
ἔτι σοι τοῦ Βρομίου μελήσει.

οἴαν οἴαν ὀργὰν
ἀναφαίνει χθόνιον
γένος ἐκφύς τε δράκοντός
ποτε Πενθεύς, ὃν Ἐχίων   540
ἐφύτευσε χθόνιος,
ἀγριωπὸν τέρας, οὐ φῶ-
τα βρότειον, φόνιον δ' ὥστε γίγαντ' ἀντίπαλον θεοῖς·
ὃς ἀμ' ἐν βρόχοισι τὰν τοῦ   545
Βρομίου τάχα ξυνάψει,
τὸν ἐμὸν δ' ἐντὸς ἀχει δώ-
ματος ἤδη θιασώταν
σκοτίαις κρυπτὸν ἐν εἱρκταῖς.
ἐσορᾷς τάδ', ὦ Διὸς παῖ   550
Διόνυσε, σοὺς προφάτας
ἐν ἁμίλλαισιν ἀνάγκας;
μόλε, χρυσῶπα τινάσσων,
ἄνα, θύρσον κατ' Ὄλυμπον,
φονίου δ' ἀνδρὸς ὕβριν κατάσχες.   555

πόθι Νύσας ἄρα τᾶς θη-
ροτρόφου θυρσοφορεῖς
θιάσους, ὦ Διόνυσ', ἢ
κορυφαῖς Κωρυκίαις;
τάχα δ' ἐν ταῖς πολυδένδρεσ-   560
σιν Ὀλύμπου θαλάμαις, ἔν-
θα ποτ' Ὀρφεὺς κιθαρίζων
σύναγεν δένδρεα μούσαις,
σύναγεν θῆρας ἀγρώτας.
μάκαρ ὦ Πιερία,   565
σέβεταί σ' Εὔιος, ἥξει

46

Why push me away?
Why seek to flee from me?
I tell you, you'll find joy
in grape-filled vines from Dionysus.
They'll make you love him.

What rage, what rage
shows up in that earth-bound race
of Pentheus, born to Echion,   [540]
an earth-bound mortal.
He's descended from a snake,
that Pentheus, a savage beast,
not a normal mortal man,
but some bloody monster
who fights against the gods.[11]
He'll soon bind me in chains,
as a worshipper of Bacchus.
Already he holds in his house
my fellow Bacchic revelers,
hidden there in some dark cell.
Do you see, Dionysus,
child of Zeus, your followers   [550]
fighting their oppression?
Come down, my lord,
down from Olympus,
wave your golden thyrsus,
to cut short the profanities
of this blood-thirsty man.

Where on Mount Nysa,
which nourishes wild beasts,
where on the Corcyrean heights,
where do you wave your thyrsus
over your worshippers,
O Dionysus?
Perhaps in those thick woods   [560]
of Mount Olympus,
where Orpheus once played his lyre,
brought trees together with his songs,
collecting wild beasts round him.
O blessed Peiria,
whom Dionysus loves —

τε χορεύσων ἅμα βακχεύ-
μασι, τόν τ᾽ ὠκυρόαν
διαβὰς Ἀξιὸν εἱλισ-
σομένας Μαινάδας ἄξει,   570
Λυδίαν πατέρα τε, τὸν
τᾶς εὐδαιμονίας βροτοῖς
ὀλβοδόταν, τὸν ἔκλυον
εὔιππον χώραν ὕδασιν
καλλίστοισι λιπαίνειν.   575

ΔΙΟΝΥΣΟΣ
  ἰώ,
  κλύετ᾽ ἐμᾶς κλύετ᾽ αὐδᾶς,
  ἰὼ βάκχαι, ἰὼ βάκχαι.

ΧΟΡΟΣ
  τίς ὅδε, τίς ὅδε πόθεν ὁ κέλαδος
  ἀνά μ᾽ ἐκάλεσεν Εὐίου;

ΔΙΟΝΥΣΟΣ
  ἰὼ ἰώ, πάλιν αὐδῶ,   580
  ὁ Σεμέλας, ὁ Διὸς παῖς.

ΧΟΡΟΣ
  ἰὼ ἰὼ δέσποτα δέσποτα,
  μόλε νυν ἡμέτερον ἐς
  θίασον, ὦ Βρόμιε Βρόμιε.

ΔΙΟΝΥΣΟΣ
  σεῖε πέδον χθονὸς Ἔννοσι πότνια.   585

ΧΟΡΟΣ
  ἆ ἆ,
  τάχα τὰ Πενθέως μέλαθρα διατι-
  νάξεται πεσήμασιν.

  — ὁ Διόνυσος ἀνὰ μέλαθρα·
  σέβετέ νιν.   590

  — σέβομεν ὤ.

48

he'll come to set you dancing
in the Bacchic celebrations.
He'll cross the foaming Axius,
lead his whirling Maenads on,   [570]
leaving behind the river Lydias
which enriches mortal men,
and which, they say, acts as a father,
nourishing with many lovely streams
a land where horses flourish.

*[The soldiers move in to round up the chorus of Bacchae. As they do so, the
ground begins to shake, thunder sounds, lightning flashes, and the entire palace
starts to break apart]*

DIONYSUS *[shouting from within the palace]*
Io! Hear me, hear me as I call you.
Io! Bacchae! Io Bacchae!

CHORUS *[a confusion of different voices in the following speeches]*
Who's that? Who is it? It's Dionysus' voice!
It's calling me. But from what direction?

DIONYSUS *[from inside the palace]*
Io! Io! I'm calling out again—   [580]
the son of Semele, a child of Zeus!

CHORUS
Io! Io! Lord and master!
Come join our company,
Bromius, oh Bromius!

DIONYSUS *[from inside]*
Sacred lord of earthquakes, shake this ground.

[The earthquake tremors resume]

CHORUS VOICE 1
Ai! Soon Pentheus' palace
will be shaken into rubble.

CHORUS VOICE 2
Dionysus is in the house—revere him.

CHORUS VOICE 3
We revere him, we revere him.   [590]

49

— εἴδετε λάινα κίοσιν ἔμβολα
διάδρομα τάδε; Βρόμιος ὅδ᾽ ἀλα-
λάζεται στέγας ἔσω.

ΔΙΟΝΥΣΟΣ

ἅπτε κεραύνιον αἴθοπα λαμπάδα·
σύμφλεγε σύμφλεγε δώματα Πενθέος.   595

ΧΟΡΟΣ

ἆ ἆ,
πῦρ οὐ λεύσσεις, οὐδ᾽ αὐγάζῃ,
Σεμέλας ἱερὸν ἀμφὶ τάφον, ἅν
ποτε κεραυνόβολος ἔλιπε φλόγα
Δίου βροντᾶς;
δίκετε πεδόσε τρομερὰ σώματα   600
δίκετε, Μαινάδες· ὁ γὰρ ἄναξ
ἄνω κάτω τιθεὶς ἔπεισι
μέλαθρα τάδε Διὸς γόνος.

ΔΙΟΝΥΣΟΣ

βάρβαροι γυναῖκες, οὕτως ἐκπεπληγμέναι φόβῳ
πρὸς πέδῳ πεπτώκατ᾽; ᾔσθησθ᾽, ὡς ἔοικε, Βακχίου   605
διατινάξαντος ‘ δῶμα Πενθέως· ἀλλ᾽ ἐξανίστατε ’
σῶμα καὶ θαρσεῖτε σαρκὸς ἐξαμείψασαι τρόμον.

ΧΟΡΟΣ

ὦ φάος μέγιστον ἡμῖν εὐίου βακχεύματος,
ὡς ἐσεῖδον ἀσμένη σε, μονάδ᾽ ἔχουσ᾽ ἐρημίαν.

ΔΙΟΝΥΣΟΣ

εἰς ἀθυμίαν ἀφίκεσθ᾽, ἡνίκ᾽ εἰσεπεμπόμην,   610
Πενθέως ὡς ἐς σκοτεινὰς ὁρκάνας πεσούμενος;

ΧΟΡΟΣ

πῶς γὰρ οὔ; τίς μοι φύλαξ ἦν, εἰ σὺ συμφορᾶς τύχοις;
ἀλλὰ πῶς ἠλευθερώθης ἀνδρὸς ἀνοσίου τυχών;

CHORUS VOICE 4

You see those stone lintels on the pillars—
they're splitting up. It's Bromius calling,
shouting to us from inside the walls.

DIONYSUS *[from inside the palace]*

Let fiery lightning strike right now—
burn Pentheus' palace—consume it all!

CHORUS VOICE 5

Look! Don't you see the fire—
there by the sacred tomb of Semele!
The flame left by that thunderbolt from Zeus,
when the lightning flash destroyed her,
all that time ago. Oh Maenads—
throw your bodies on the ground, down, down,   [600]
for our master, Zeus' son, moves now
against the palace—to demolish it.

*[Enter Dionysus, bursting through the palace front doors, free of all chains,
smiling and supremely confident.]*

DIONYSUS

Ah, my barbarian Asian women,
Do you lie there on the ground prostrate with fear?
It seems you feel Dionysus' power,
as he rattles Pentheus' palace.
Get up now. Be brave. And stop your trembling.

CHORUS LEADER

How happy I am to see you—
Our greatest light in all the joyful dancing.
We felt alone and totally abandoned.

DIONYSUS

Did you feel despair when I was sent away,   [610]
cast down in Pentheus' gloomy dungeon?

CHORUS LEADER

How could I not? Who'll protect me
if you run into trouble? But tell me,
how did you escape that ungodly man?

Euripides

ΔΙΟΝΥΣΟΣ

αὐτὸς ἐξέσῳσ᾽ ἐμαυτὸν ῥᾳδίως ἄνευ πόνου.

ΧΟΡΟΣ

οὐδέ σου συνῆψε χεῖρε δεσμίοισιν ἐν βρόχοις;   615

ΔΙΟΝΥΣΟΣ

ταῦτα καὶ καθύβρισ᾽ αὐτόν, ὅτι με δεσμεύειν δοκῶν
οὔτ᾽ ἔθιγεν οὔθ᾽ ἥψαθ᾽ ἡμῶν, ἐλπίσιν δ᾽ ἐβόσκετο.
πρὸς φάτναις δὲ ταῦρον εὑρών, οὗ καθεῖρξ᾽ ἡμᾶς ἄγων,
τῷδε περὶ βρόχους ἔβαλλε γόνασι καὶ χηλαῖς ποδῶν,
θυμὸν ἐκπνέων, ἱδρῶτα σώματος στάζων ἄπο,   620
χείλεσιν διδοὺς ὀδόντας· πλησίον δ᾽ ἐγὼ παρὼν
ἥσυχος θάσσων ἔλευσσον. ἐν δὲ τῷδε τῷ χρόνῳ
ἀνετίναξ᾽ ἐλθὼν ὁ Βάκχος δῶμα καὶ μητρὸς τάφῳ
πῦρ ἀνῆψ᾽· ὁ δ᾽ ὡς ἐσεῖδε, δώματ᾽ αἴθεσθαι δοκῶν,
ᾖσσ᾽ ἐκεῖσε κᾆτ᾽ ἐκεῖσε, δμωσὶν Ἀχελῷον φέρειν   625
ἐννέπων, ἅπας δ᾽ ἐν ἔργῳ δοῦλος ἦν, μάτην πονῶν.
διαμεθεὶς δὲ τόνδε μόχθον, ὡς ἐμοῦ πεφευγότος,
ἵεται ξίφος κελαινὸν ἁρπάσας δόμων ἔσω.
κᾆθ᾽ ὁ Βρόμιος, ὡς ἔμοιγε φαίνεται, δόξαν λέγω,
φάσμ᾽ ἐποίησεν κατ᾽ αὐλήν· ὁ δ᾽ ἐπὶ τοῦθ᾽ ὡρμημένος 630
ᾖσσε κἀκέντει φαεννὸν αἰθέρ᾽, ὡς σφάζων ἐμέ.
πρὸς δὲ τοῖσδ᾽ αὐτῷ τάδ᾽ ἄλλα Βάκχιος λυμαίνεται·
δώματ᾽ ἔρρηξεν χαμᾶζε· συντεθράνωται δ᾽ ἅπαν
πικροτάτους ἰδόντι δεσμοὺς τοὺς ἐμούς· κόπου δ᾽ ὕπο
διαμεθεὶς ξίφος παρεῖται· πρὸς θεὸν γὰρ ὢν ἀνὴρ   635
ἐς μάχην ἐλθεῖν ἐτόλμησε. ἥσυχος δ᾽ ἐκβὰς ἐγὼ
δωμάτων ἥκω πρὸς ὑμᾶς, Πενθέως οὐ φροντίσας.
ὡς δέ μοι δοκεῖ—ψοφεῖ γοῦν ἀρβύλη δόμων ἔσω—
ἐς προνώπι᾽ αὐτίχ᾽ ἥξει. τί ποτ᾽ ἄρ᾽ ἐκ τούτων ἐρεῖ;

52

DIONYSUS

    No trouble. I saved myself with ease.

CHORUS LEADER

    But didn't he bind up your hands up in chains?

DIONYSUS

    In this business I was playing with him —
    he thought he was tying me up, the fool!
    He didn't even touch or handle me,
    he was so busy feeding his desires.
    In that stable where he went to tie me up,
    he found a bull. He threw the iron fetters
    around its knees and hooves. As he did so,
    he kept panting in his rage, dripping sweat   [620]
    from his whole body — his teeth gnawed his lip.
    I watched him, sitting quietly nearby.
    After a while, Bacchus came and shook the place,
    setting his mother Semele's tomb on fire.
    Seeing that, Pentheus thought his palace
    was burning down. He ran round, here and there,
    yelling to his slaves to bring more water.
    His servants set to work — and all for nothing!
    Once I'd escaped, he ended all that work.
    Seizing a dark sword, he rushed inside the house.
    Then, it seems to me, but I'm guessing now,
    Bromius set up out there in the courtyard   [630]
    some phantom image. Pentheus charged it,
    slashing away at nothing but bright air,
    thinking he was butchering me. There's more —
    Bacchus kept hurting him in still more ways.
    He knocked his house down, right to the ground,
    all shattered, so Pentheus has witnessed
    a bitter end to my imprisonment.
    He's dropped his sword, worn out, exhausted,
    a mere mortal daring to fight a god.
    So now I've strolled out calmly to you,
    leaving the house, ignoring Pentheus.
    Wait! It seems to me I hear marching feet —
    no doubt he'll come out front here soon enough.
    What will he say, I wonder, after this?

ῥᾳδίως γὰρ αὐτὸν οἴσω, κἂν πνέων ἔλθῃ μέγα. 640
πρὸς σοφοῦ γὰρ ἀνδρὸς ἀσκεῖν σώφρον᾽ εὐοργησίαν.

ΠΕΝΘΕΥΣ

πέπονθα δεινά· διαπέφευγέ μ᾽ ὁ ξένος,
ὃς ἄρτι δεσμοῖς ἦν κατηναγκασμένος.
ἔα ἔα·
ὅδ᾽ ἐστὶν ἀνήρ· τί τάδε; πῶς προνώπιος 645
φαίνῃ πρὸς οἴκοις τοῖς ἐμοῖς, ἔξω βεβώς;

ΔΙΟΝΥΣΟΣ

στῆσον πόδ᾽, ὀργῇ δ᾽ ὑπόθες ἥσυχον πόδα.

ΠΕΝΘΕΥΣ

πόθεν σὺ δεσμὰ διαφυγὼν ἔξω περᾷς;

ΔΙΟΝΥΣΟΣ

οὐκ εἶπον—ἢ οὐκ ἤκουσας—ὅτι λύσει μέ τις;

ΠΕΝΘΕΥΣ

τίς; τοὺς λόγους γὰρ ἐσφέρεις καινοὺς ἀεί. 650

ΔΙΟΝΥΣΟΣ

ὃς τὴν πολύβοτρυν ἄμπελον φύει βροτοῖς.

ΠΕΝΘΕΥΣ

<...>

ΔΙΟΝΥΣΟΣ

ὠνείδισας δὴ τοῦτο Διονύσῳ καλόν.

ΠΕΝΘΕΥΣ

κλῄειν κελεύω πάντα πύργον ἐν κύκλῳ.

ΔΙΟΝΥΣΟΣ

τί δ᾽; οὐχ ὑπερβαίνουσι καὶ τείχη θεοί;

Well, I'll deal with him quite gently, [640]
even if he comes out breathing up a storm.
After all, a wise man ought to keep his temper.

[Pentheus comes hurriedly out of the palace, accompanied by armed soldiers]

PENTHEUS

What's happening to me—total disaster!
The stranger's escaped, and we'd just chained him up.

[seeing Dionysus]

Ah ha! Here is the man—right here.
What's going on? How did you get out?
How come you're here, outside my palace?

DIONYSUS

Hold on. Calm down. Don't be so angry.

PENTHEUS

How did you escape your chains and get here?

DIONYSUS

Didn't I say someone would release me—
or did you miss that part?

PENTHEUS

                                                  Who was it? [650]
You're always explaining things in riddles.

DIONYSUS

It was the one who cultivates for men
the richly clustering vine.

PENTHEUS

                                        Ah, this Dionysus.
Your words are a lovely insult to your god.

DIONYSUS

He came to Thebes with nothing but good things.

PENTHEUS *[to soldiers]*

Seal off all the towers on my orders—
all of them around the city.

DIONYSUS

                                    What for?
Surely a god can make it over any wall?

55

ΠΕΝΘΕΥΣ

σοφὸς σοφὸς σύ, πλὴν ἃ δεῖ σ᾽ εἶναι σοφόν.   655

ΔΙΟΝΥΣΟΣ

ἃ δεῖ μάλιστα, ταῦτ᾽ ἔγωγ᾽ ἔφυν σοφός.

κείνου δ᾽ ἀκούσας πρῶτα τοὺς λόγους μάθε,
ὃς ἐξ ὄρους πάρεστιν ἀγγελῶν τί σοι·
ἡμεῖς δέ σοι μενοῦμεν, οὐ φευξούμεθα.

ΑΓΓΕΛΟΣ

Πενθεῦ κρατύνων τῆσδε Θηβαίας χθονός,   660
ἥκω Κιθαιρῶν᾽ ἐκλιπών, ἵν᾽ οὔποτε
λευκῆς χιόνος ἀνεῖσαν εὐαγεῖς βολαί.

ΠΕΝΘΕΥΣ

ἥκεις δὲ ποίαν προστιθεὶς σπουδὴν λόγου;

ΑΓΓΕΛΟΣ

βάκχας ποτνιάδας εἰσιδών, αἳ τῆσδε γῆς
οἴστροισι λευκὸν κῶλον ἐξηκόντισαν,   665
ἥκω φράσαι σοὶ καὶ πόλει χρῄζων, ἄναξ,
ὡς δεινὰ δρῶσι θαυμάτων τε κρείσσονα.
θέλω δ᾽ ἀκοῦσαι, πότερά σοι παρρησίᾳ
φράσω τὰ κεῖθεν ἢ λόγον στειλώμεθα·
τὸ γὰρ τάχος σου τῶν φρενῶν δέδοικ᾽, ἄναξ,   670
καὶ τοὐξύθυμον καὶ τὸ βασιλικὸν λίαν.

ΠΕΝΘΕΥΣ

λέγ᾽, ὡς ἀθῷος ἐξ ἐμοῦ πάντως ἔσῃ.
τοῖς γὰρ δικαίοις οὐχὶ θυμοῦσθαι χρεών.
ὅσῳ δ᾽ ἂν εἴπῃς δεινότερα βακχῶν πέρι,
τοσῷδε μᾶλλον τὸν ὑποθέντα τὰς τέχνας   675
γυναιξὶ τόνδε τῇ δίκῃ προσθήσομεν.

PENTHEUS

    You're so wise, except in all those things
    in which you should be wise.

DIONYSUS

                     I was born wise,
    especially in matters where I need to be.

[Enter the Messenger, a cattle herder from the hills]

DIONYSUS

    But first you'd better listen to this man,
    hear what he has to say, for he's come here
    from the mountains to report to you.
    I'll still be here for you. I won't run off.

MESSENGER

    Pentheus, ruler of this land of Thebes,   [660]
    I've just left Cithaeron, that mountain
    where the sparkling snow never melts away.

PENTHEUS

    What this important news you've come with?

MESSENGER

    I saw those women in their Bacchic revels,
    those sacred screamers, all driven crazy,
    the ones who run barefoot from their homes.
    I came, my lord, to tell you and the city
    the dreadful things they're doing, their actions
    are beyond all wonder. But, my lord,
    first I wish to know if I should tell you,
    openly report what's going on up there,
    or whether I should hold my tongue.
    Your mood changes so fast I get afraid—   [670]
    your sharp spirit, your all-too-royal temper.

PENTHEUS

    Speak on. Whatever you have to report,
    you'll get no punishment at all from me.
    It's not right to vent one's anger on the just.
    The more terrible the things you tell me
    about those Bacchic women, the worse
    I'll move against the one who taught them
    all their devious tricks.

Euripides

ἌΓΓΕΛΟΣ
ἀγελαῖα μὲν βοσκήματ' ἄρτι πρὸς λέπας
μόσχων ὑπεξήκριζον, ἡνίχ' ἥλιος
ἀκτῖνας ἐξίησι θερμαίνων χθόνα.
ὁρῶ δὲ θιάσους τρεῖς γυναικείων χορῶν,   680
ὧν ἦρχ' ἑνὸς μὲν Αὐτονόη, τοῦ δευτέρου
μήτηρ Ἀγαύη σή, τρίτου δ' Ἰνὼ χοροῦ.
ηὖδον δὲ πᾶσαι σώμασιν παρειμέναι,
αἳ μὲν πρὸς ἐλάτης νῶτ' ἐρείσασαι φόβην,
αἳ δ' ἐν δρυὸς φύλλοισι πρὸς πέδῳ κάρα   685
εἰκῇ βαλοῦσαι σωφρόνως, οὐχ ὡς σὺ φῂς
ᾠνωμένας κρατῆρι καὶ λωτοῦ ψόφῳ
θηρᾶν καθ' ὕλην Κύπριν ἠρημωμένας.
ἡ σὴ δὲ μήτηρ ὠλόλυξεν ἐν μέσαις
σταθεῖσα βάκχαις, ἐξ ὕπνου κινεῖν δέμας,   690
μυκήμαθ' ὡς ἤκουσε κεροφόρων βοῶν.
αἳ δ' ἀποβαλοῦσαι θαλερὸν ὀμμάτων ὕπνον
ἀνῇξαν ὀρθαί, θαῦμ' ἰδεῖν εὐκοσμίας,
νέαι παλαιαὶ παρθένοι τ' ἔτ' ἄζυγες.
καὶ πρῶτα μὲν καθεῖσαν εἰς ὤμους κόμας   695
νεβρίδας τ' ἀνεστείλανθ' ὅσαισιν ἀμμάτων
σύνδεσμ' ἐλέλυτο, καὶ καταστίκτους δορὰς
ὄφεσι κατεζώσαντο λιχμῶσιν γένυν.
αἳ δ' ἀγκάλαισι δορκάδ' ἢ σκύμνους λύκων
ἀγρίους ἔχουσαι λευκὸν ἐδίδοσαν γάλα,   700
ὅσαις νεοτόκοις μαστὸς ἦν σπαργῶν ἔτι
βρέφη λιπούσαις· ἐπὶ δ' ἔθεντο κισσίνους
στεφάνους δρυός τε μίλακός τ' ἀνθεσφόρου.
θύρσον δέ τις λαβοῦσ' ἔπαισεν ἐς πέτραν,
ὅθεν δροσώδης ὕδατος ἐκπηδᾷ νοτίς·   705
ἄλλη δὲ νάρθηκ' ἐς πέδον καθῆκε γῆς,
καὶ τῇδε κρήνην ἐξανῆκ' οἴνου θεός·
ὅσαις δὲ λευκοῦ πώματος πόθος παρῆν,
ἄκροισι δακτύλοισι διαμῶσαι χθόνα
γάλακτος ἑσμοὺς εἶχον· ἐκ δὲ κισσίνων   710
θύρσων γλυκεῖαι μέλιτος ἔσταζον ῥοαί.

58

MESSENGER

                       The grazing cattle
were just moving into upland pastures,
at the hour the sun sends out its beams
to warm the earth. Right then I saw them —
three groups of dancing women. One of them   [680]
Autonoe led. Your mother, Agave,
led the second group, and Ino led the third.
They were all asleep, bodies quite relaxed,
some leaning back on leafy boughs of pine,
others cradling heads on oak-leaf pillows,
resting on the ground — in all modesty.
They weren't as you described — all drunk on wine
or on the music of their flutes, hunting
for Aphrodite in the woods alone.
Once she heard my horned cattle lowing,
your mother stood up amid those Bacchae,
then called them to stir their limbs from sleep.
They rubbed refreshing sleep out of their eyes,   [690]
and stood up straight there — a marvelous sight,
to see such an orderly arrangement,
women young and old and still unmarried girls.
First, they let their hair loose down their shoulders,
tied up the fawn skins (some had untied the knots
to loosen up the chords). Then around those skins
they looped some snakes, who licked the women's cheeks.
Some held young gazelles or wild wolf cubs
and fed them on their own white milk, the ones   [700]
who'd left behind at home a new-born child
whose breasts were still swollen full of milk.
They draped themselves with garlands from oak trees,
ivy and flowering yew. Then one of them,
taking a thyrsus, struck a rock with it,
and water gushed out, fresh as dew. Another,
using her thyrsus, scraped the ground. At once,
the god sent fountains of wine up from the spot.
All those who craved white milk to drink
just scratched the earth with their fingertips —
it came out in streams. From their ivy wands   [710]
thick sweet honey dripped. Oh, if you'd been there,

ὥστ', εἰ παρῆσθα, τὸν θεὸν τὸν νῦν ψέγεις
εὐχαῖσιν ἂν μετῆλθες εἰσιδὼν τάδε.
ξυνήλθομεν δὲ βουκόλοι καὶ ποιμένες,
κοινῶν λόγων δώσοντες ἀλλήλοις ἔριν   715
ὡς δεινὰ δρῶσι θαυμάτων τ' ἐπάξια·
καί τις πλάνης κατ' ἄστυ καὶ τρίβων λόγων
ἔλεξεν εἰς ἅπαντας· Ὦ σεμνὰς πλάκας
ναίοντες ὀρέων, θέλετε θηρασώμεθα
Πενθέως Ἀγαύην μητέρ' ἐκ βακχευμάτων   720
χάριν τ' ἄνακτι θώμεθα; εὖ δ' ἡμῖν λέγειν
ἔδοξε, θάμνων δ' ἐλλοχίζομεν φόβαις
κρύψαντες αὑτούς· αἱ δὲ τὴν τεταγμένην
ὥραν ἐκίνουν θύρσον ἐς βακχεύματα,
Ἴακχον ἀθρόῳ στόματι τὸν Διὸς γόνον   725
Βρόμιον καλοῦσαι· πᾶν δὲ συνεβάκχευ' ὄρος
καὶ θῆρες, οὐδὲν δ' ἦν ἀκίνητον δρόμῳ.
κυρεῖ δ' Ἀγαύη πλησίον θρῴσκουσά μου·
κἀγὼ 'ξεπήδησ' ὡς συναρπάσαι θέλων,
λόχμην κενώσας ἔνθ' ἐκρυπτόμην δέμας.   730
ἡ δ' ἀνεβόησεν· Ὦ δρομάδες ἐμαὶ κύνες,
θηρώμεθ' ἀνδρῶν τῶνδ' ὕπ'· ἀλλ' ἕπεσθέ μοι,
ἕπεσθε θύρσοις διὰ χερῶν ὡπλισμέναι.
ἡμεῖς μὲν οὖν φεύγοντες ἐξηλύξαμεν
βακχῶν σπαραγμόν, αἱ δὲ νεμομέναις χλόην   735
μόσχοις ἐπῆλθον χειρὸς ἀσιδήρου μέτα.
καὶ τὴν μὲν ἂν προσεῖδες εὔθηλον πόριν
μυκωμένην ἔχουσαν ἐν χεροῖν δίχα,
ἄλλαι δὲ δαμάλας διεφόρουν σπαράγμασιν.
εἶδες δ' ἂν ἢ πλεύρ' ἢ δίχηλον ἔμβασιν   740
ῥιπτόμεν' ἄνω τε καὶ κάτω· κρεμαστὰ δὲ
ἔσταζ' ὑπ' ἐλάταις ἀναπεφυρμέν' αἵματι.
ταῦροι δ' ὑβρισταὶ κἀς κέρας θυμούμενοι
τὸ πρόσθεν ἐσφάλλοντο πρὸς γαῖαν δέμας,
μυριάσι χειρῶν ἀγόμενοι νεανίδων.   745
θᾶσσον δὲ διεφοροῦντο σαρκὸς ἐνδυτὰ
ἢ σὲ ξυνάψαι βλέφαρα βασιλείοις κόραις.

if you'd seen this, you'd come with reverence
to that god whom you criticize so much.
Well, we cattle herders and shepherds met
to discuss and argue with each other
about the astonishing things we'd seen.
And then a man who'd been in town a bit
and had a way with words said to us all,
"You men who live in the holy regions
of these mountains, how'd you like to hunt down
Pentheus' mother, Agave — take her   [720]
away from these Bacchic celebrations,
do the king a favour?" To all of us
he seemed to make good sense. So we set up
an ambush, hiding in the bushes,
lying down there. At the appointed time,
the women started their Bacchic ritual,
brandishing the thyrsus and calling out
to the god they cry to, Bromius, Zeus' son.
The entire mountain and its wild animals
were, like them, in one Bacchic ecstasy.
As these women moved, they made all things dance.
Agave, by chance, was dancing close to me.
Leaving the ambush where I'd been concealed,
I jumped out, hoping to grab hold of her.   [730]
But she screamed out, "Oh, my quick hounds,
men are hunting us. Come, follow me.
Come on, armed with that thyrsus in your hand."
We ran off, and so escaped being torn apart.
But then those Bacchic women, all unarmed,
went at the heifers browsing on the turf,
using their bare hands. You should have seen one
ripping a fat, young, lowing calf apart —
others tearing cows in pieces with their hands.
You could've seen ribs and cloven hooves   [740]
tossed everywhere — some hung up in branches
dripping blood and gore. And bulls, proud beasts till then,
with angry horns, collapsed there on the ground,
dragged down by the hands of a thousand girls.
Hides covering their bodies were stripped off
faster than you could wink your royal eye.

Euripides

χωροῦσι δ' ὥστ' ὄρνιθες ἀρθεῖσαι δρόμῳ
πεδίων ὑποτάσεις, αἳ παρ' Ἀσωποῦ ῥοαῖς
εὔκαρπον ἐκβάλλουσι Θηβαίων στάχυν·
Ὑσιάς τ' Ἐρυθράς θ', αἳ Κιθαιρῶνος λέπας
νέρθεν κατῳκήκασιν, ὥστε πολέμιοι,
ἐπεσπεσοῦσαι πάντ' ἄνω τε καὶ κάτω
διέφερον· ἥρπαζον μὲν ἐκ δόμων τέκνα·
ὁπόσα δ' ἐπ' ὤμοις ἔθεσαν, οὐ δεσμῶν ὕπο
προσείχετ' οὐδ' ἔπιπτεν ἐς μέλαν πέδον,
οὐ χαλκός, οὐ σίδηρος· ἐπὶ δὲ βοστρύχοις
πῦρ ἔφερον, οὐδ' ἔκαιεν. οἱ δ' ὀργῆς ὕπο
ἐς ὅπλ' ἐχώρουν φερόμενοι βακχῶν ὕπο·
οὗπερ τὸ δεινὸν ἦν θέαμ' ἰδεῖν, ἄναξ.
τοῖς μὲν γὰρ οὐχ ἥμασσε λογχωτὸν βέλος,
κεῖναι δὲ θύρσους ἐξανιεῖσαι χερῶν
ἐτραυμάτιζον κἀπενώτιζον φυγῇ
γυναῖκες ἄνδρας, οὐκ ἄνευ θεῶν τινος.
πάλιν δ' ἐχώρουν ὅθεν ἐκίνησαν πόδα,
κρήνας ἐπ' αὐτὰς ἃς ἀνῆκ' αὐταῖς θεός.
νίψαντο δ' αἷμα, σταγόνα δ' ἐκ παρηίδων
γλώσσῃ δράκοντες ἐξεφαίδρυνον χροός.
τὸν δαίμον' οὖν τόνδ' ὅστις ἔστ', ὦ δέσποτα,
δέχου πόλει τῇδ'· ὡς τά τ' ἄλλ' ἐστὶν μέγας,
κἀκεῖνό φασιν αὐτόν, ὡς ἐγὼ κλύω,
τὴν παυσίλυπον ἄμπελον δοῦναι βροτοῖς.
οἴνου δὲ μηκέτ' ὄντος οὐκ ἔστιν Κύπρις
οὐδ' ἄλλο τερπνὸν οὐδὲν ἀνθρώποις ἔτι.

ΧΟΡΟΣ
ταρβῶ μὲν εἰπεῖν τοὺς λόγους ἐλευθέρους
πρὸς τὸν τύραννον, ἀλλ' ὅμως εἰρήσεται·
Διόνυσος ἥσσων οὐδενὸς θεῶν ἔφυ.

ΠΕΝΘΕΥΣ
ἤδη τόδ' ἐγγὺς ὥστε πῦρ ὑφάπτεται
ὕβρισμα βακχῶν, ψόγος ἐς Ἕλληνας μέγας.

62

Then, like birds carried up by their own speed,
they rushed along the lower level ground,
beside Asopus' streams, that fertile land
which yields its crops to Thebes. Like fighting troops,   [750]
they raided Hysiae and Erythrae,
below rocky Cithaeron, smashing
everything, snatching children from their homes.
Whatever they carried their shoulders,
even bronze or iron, never tumbled off
onto the dark earth, though nothing was tied down.
They carried fire in their hair, but those flames
never singed them. Some of the villagers,
enraged at being plundered by the Bacchae,
seized weapons. The sight of what happened next,   [760]
my lord, was dreadful. For their pointed spears
did not draw blood. But when those women
threw the thyrsoi in their hands, they wounded them
and drove them back in flight. The women did this
to men, but not without some god's assistance.
Then they went back to where they'd started from,
those fountains which the god had made for them.
They washed off the blood. Snakes licked their cheeks,
cleansing their skin of every drop. My lord,
you must welcome this god into our city,
whoever he is. He's a mighty god   [770]
in many other ways. The people say,
so I've heard, he gives to mortal human beings
that vine which puts an end to human grief.
Without wine, there's no more Aphrodite—
or any other pleasure left for men.

CHORUS LEADER

I'm afraid to talk freely before the king,
but nonetheless I'll speak—this Dionysus
is not inferior to any god.

PENTHEUS

This Dionysian arrogance, like fire,
keeps flaring up close by—a great insult
to all the Greeks. We must not hesitate.

ἀλλ' οὐκ ὀκνεῖν δεῖ· στεῖχ' ἐπ' Ἠλέκτρας ἰὼν   780
πύλας· κέλευε πάντας ἀσπιδηφόρους
ἵππων τ' ἀπαντᾶν ταχυπόδων ἐπεμβάτας
πέλτας θ' ὅσοι πάλλουσι καὶ τόξων χερὶ
ψάλλουσι νευράς, ὡς ἐπιστρατεύσομεν
βάκχαισιν· οὐ γὰρ ἀλλ' ὑπερβάλλει τάδε,   785
εἰ πρὸς γυναικῶν πεισόμεσθ' ἃ πάσχομεν.

ΔΙΟΝΥΣΟΣ
πείθῃ μὲν οὐδέν, τῶν ἐμῶν λόγων κλύων,
Πενθεῦ· κακῶς δὲ πρὸς σέθεν πάσχων ὅμως
οὔ φημι χρῆναί σ' ὅπλ' ἐπαίρεσθαι θεῷ,
ἀλλ' ἡσυχάζειν· Βρόμιος οὐκ ἀνέξεται   790
κινοῦντα βάκχας σ' εὐίων ὀρῶν ἄπο.

ΠΕΝΘΕΥΣ
οὐ μὴ φρενώσεις μ', ἀλλὰ δέσμιος φυγὼν
σώσῃ τόδ'; ἢ σοὶ πάλιν ἀναστρέψω δίκην;

ΔΙΟΝΥΣΟΣ
θύοιμ' ἂν αὐτῷ μᾶλλον ἢ θυμούμενος
πρὸς κέντρα λακτίζοιμι θνητὸς ὢν θεῷ.   795

ΠΕΝΘΕΥΣ
θύσω, φόνον γε θῆλυν, ὥσπερ ἄξιαι,
πολὺν ταράξας ἐν Κιθαιρῶνος πτυχαῖς.

ΔΙΟΝΥΣΟΣ
φεύξεσθε πάντες· καὶ τόδ' αἰσχρόν, ἀσπίδας
θύρσοισι βακχῶν ἐκτρέπειν χαλκηλάτους

ΠΕΝΘΕΥΣ
ἀπόρῳ γε τῷδε συμπεπλέγμεθα ξένῳ,   800
ὃς οὔτε πάσχων οὔτε δρῶν σιγήσεται.

ΔΙΟΝΥΣΟΣ
ὦ τᾶν, ἔτ' ἔστιν εὖ καταστῆσαι τάδε.

[To one of his armed attendants]

Go to the Electra Gates. Call out the troops,   [780]
the heavy infantry, all fast cavalry.
Tell them to muster, along with all those
who carry shields—all the archers, too,
the men who pull the bowstring back by hand.
We'll march out against these Bacchae.
In this whole business we will lose control,
if we have to put up with what we've suffered
from these women.

DIONYSUS

                    You've heard what I had to say,
Pentheus, but still you're not convinced.
Though I'm suffering badly at your hands,
I say you shouldn't go to war against a god.
You should stay calm. Bromius will not let you   [790]
move his Bacchae from their mountains.

PENTHEUS

Don't preach to me! You've got out of prison—
enjoy that fact. Or shall I punish you some more?

DIONYSUS

I'd sooner make an offering to that god
than in some angry fit kick at his whip—
a mortal going to battle with a god.

PENTHEUS

I'll sacrifice all right—with a slaughter
of those women, just as they deserve—
in the forests on Cithaeron.

DIONYSUS

                                        You'll all run.
What a disgrace! To turn your bronze shields round,
fleeing the thyrsoi of those Bacchic women!

PENTHEUS *[turning to one of his armed attendants, as if to go]*
It's useless trying to argue with this stranger—   [800]
whatever he does or suffers, he won't shut up.

DIONYSUS *[calling Pentheus back]*
My lord! There's still a chance to end this calmly.

ΠΕΝΘΕΥΣ

τί δρῶντα; δουλεύοντα δουλείαις ἐμαῖς;

ΔΙΟΝΥΣΟΣ

ἐγὼ γυναῖκας δεῦρ' ὅπλων ἄξω δίχα.

ΠΕΝΘΕΥΣ

οἴμοι· τόδ' ἤδη δόλιον ἔς με μηχανᾷ.   805

ΔΙΟΝΥΣΟΣ

ποῖόν τι, σῶσαί σ' εἰ θέλω τέχναις ἐμαῖς;

ΠΕΝΘΕΥΣ

ξυνέθεσθε κοινῇ τάδ', ἵνα βακχεύητ' ἀεί.

ΔΙΟΝΥΣΟΣ

καὶ μὴν ξυνεθέμην—τοῦτό γ' ἔστι—τῷ θεῷ.

ΠΕΝΘΕΥΣ

ἐκφέρετέ μοι δεῦρ' ὅπλα, σὺ δὲ παῦσαι λέγων.

ΔΙΟΝΥΣΟΣ

ἆ.   810

βούλῃ σφ' ἐν ὄρεσι συγκαθημένας ἰδεῖν;

ΠΕΝΘΕΥΣ

μάλιστα, μυρίον γε δοὺς χρυσοῦ σταθμόν.

ΔΙΟΝΥΣΟΣ

τί δ' εἰς ἔρωτα τοῦδε πέπτωκας μέγαν;

ΠΕΝΘΕΥΣ

λυπρῶς νιν εἰσίδοιμ' ἂν ἐξῳνωμένας.

66

PENTHEUS

By doing what? Should I become a slave
to my own slaves?

DIONYSUS

I'll bring the women here—
without the use of any weapons.

PENTHEUS

I don't think so.
You're setting me up for your tricks again.

DIONYSUS

What sort of trick, if I want to save you
in my own way?

PENTHEUS

You've made some arrangement,
you and your god, so you can always dance
your Bacchanalian orgies.

DIONYSUS

Yes, that's true.
I have made some arrangement with the god.

PENTHEUS *[to one of his armed servants]*

You there, bring me my weapons.
[to Dionysus]

And you—
No more talk! Keep quiet!

DIONYSUS

Just a minute!   [810]

[moving up to Pentheus]
How'd you like to gaze upon those women out there,
sitting together in the mountains?

PENTHEUS

I'd like that.
Yes, for that I'd pay in gold—and pay a lot.

DIONYSUS

Why is that? Why do you desire it so much?

PENTHEUS

I'd be sorry to see the women drunk.

67

ΔΙΟΝΥΣΟΣ

ὅμως δ' ἴδοις ἂν ἡδέως ἅ σοι πικρά;   815

ΠΕΝΘΕΥΣ

σάφ' ἴσθι, σιγῇ γ' ὑπ' ἐλάταις καθήμενος.

ΔΙΟΝΥΣΟΣ

ἀλλ' ἐξιχνεύσουσίν σε, κἂν ἔλθῃς λάθρᾳ.

ΠΕΝΘΕΥΣ

ἀλλ' ἐμφανῶς· καλῶς γὰρ ἐξεῖπας τάδε.

ΔΙΟΝΥΣΟΣ

ἄγωμεν οὖν σε κἀπιχειρήσεις ὁδῷ;

ΠΕΝΘΕΥΣ

ἄγ' ὡς τάχιστα, τοῦ χρόνου δέ σοι φθονῶ.   820

ΔΙΟΝΥΣΟΣ

στεῖλαί νυν ἀμφὶ χρωτὶ βυσσίνους πέπλους.

ΠΕΝΘΕΥΣ

τί δὴ τόδ'; ἐς γυναῖκας ἐξ ἀνδρὸς τελῶ;

ΔΙΟΝΥΣΟΣ

μή σε κτάνωσιν, ἢν ἀνὴρ ὀφθῇς ἐκεῖ.

ΠΕΝΘΕΥΣ

εὖ γ' εἶπας αὖ τόδ'· ὥς τις εἶ πάλαι σοφός.

ΔΙΟΝΥΣΟΣ

Διόνυσος ἡμᾶς ἐξεμούσωσεν τάδε.   825

ΠΕΝΘΕΥΣ

πῶς οὖν γένοιτ' ἂν ἃ σύ με νουθετεῖς καλῶς;

ΔΙΟΝΥΣΟΣ

ἐγὼ στελῶ σε δωμάτων ἔσω μολών.

DIONYSUS

Would you derive pleasure from looking on,
viewing something you find painful?

PENTHEUS

                                        Yes, I would —
if I were sitting in the trees in silence.

DIONYSUS

But even if you go there secretly,
they'll track you down.

PENTHEUS

                                        You're right.
I'll go there openly.

DIONYSUS

                                        So you're prepared,
are you, to make the trip? Shall I lead you there?

PENTHEUS

Let's go, and with all speed. I've got time.   [820]

DIONYSUS

In that case, you must clothe your body
in a dress — one made of eastern linen.

PENTHEUS

What! I'm not going up there as a man?
I've got to change myself into a woman?

DIONYSUS

If they see you as a man, they'll kill you.

PENTHEUS

Right again. You always have the answer.

DIONYSUS

Dionysus taught me all these things.

PENTHEUS

How can I best follow your suggestion?

DIONYSUS

I'll go inside your house and dress you up.

69

Euripides

ΠΕΝΘΕΥΣ
τίνα στολήν; ἦ θῆλυν; ἀλλ' αἰδώς μ' ἔχει.

ΔΙΟΝΥΣΟΣ
οὐκέτι θεατὴς μαινάδων πρόθυμος εἶ.

ΠΕΝΘΕΥΣ
στολὴν δὲ τίνα φῂς ἀμφὶ χρῶτ' ἐμὸν βαλεῖν;   830

ΔΙΟΝΥΣΟΣ
κόμην μὲν ἐπὶ σῷ κρατὶ ταναὸν ἐκτενῶ.

ΠΕΝΘΕΥΣ
τὸ δεύτερον δὲ σχῆμα τοῦ κόσμου τί μοι;

ΔΙΟΝΥΣΟΣ
πέπλοι ποδήρεις· ἐπὶ κάρᾳ δ' ἔσται μίτρα.

ΠΕΝΘΕΥΣ
ἦ καί τι πρὸς τοῖσδ' ἄλλο προσθήσεις ἐμοί;

ΔΙΟΝΥΣΟΣ
θύρσον γε χειρὶ καὶ νεβροῦ στικτὸν δέρας.   835

ΠΕΝΘΕΥΣ
οὐκ ἂν δυναίμην θῆλυν ἐνδῦναι στολήν.

ΔΙΟΝΥΣΟΣ
ἀλλ' αἷμα θήσεις συμβαλὼν βάκχαις μάχην.

ΠΕΝΘΕΥΣ
ὀρθῶς· μολεῖν χρὴ πρῶτον εἰς κατασκοπήν.

ΔΙΟΝΥΣΟΣ
σοφώτερον γοῦν ἢ κακοῖς θηρᾶν κακά.

ΠΕΝΘΕΥΣ
καὶ πῶς δι' ἄστεως εἶμι Καδμείους λαθών;   840

PENTHEUS

What? Dress up in a female outfit?
I can't do that—I'd be ashamed to.

DIONYSUS

You're still keen to see the Maenads, aren't you?

PENTHEUS

What sort of clothing do you recommend?
How should I cover up my body?   [830]

DIONYSUS

I'll fix up a long hair piece for your head.

PENTHEUS

                                    All right.
What's the next piece of my outfit?

DIONYSUS

A dress down to your feet—then a headband,
to fit just here, around your forehead.

PENTHEUS

What else? What other things will you provide?

DIONYSUS

A thyrsus to hold and a dappled fawn skin.

PENTHEUS

No. I can't dress up in women's clothes!

DIONYSUS

But if you go fighting with these Bacchae,
you'll cause bloodshed.

PENTHEUS

                                    Yes, that's true.
So first, we must go up and spy on them.

DIONYSUS

Hunt down evil by committing evil—
that sounds like a wise way to proceed.

PENTHEUS

But how will I make it through the city
without the Thebans noticing me?   [840]

71

Euripides

ΔΙΟΝΥΣΟΣ
    ὁδοὺς ἐρήμους ἴμεν· ἐγὼ δ' ἡγήσομαι.

ΠΕΝΘΕΥΣ
    πᾶν κρεῖσσον ὥστε μὴ 'γγελᾶν βάκχας ἐμοί.
    ἐλθόντ' ἐς οἴκους . . . ἂν δοκῇ βουλεύσομαι.

ΔΙΟΝΥΣΟΣ
    ἔξεστι· πάντῃ τό γ' ἐμὸν εὐτρεπὲς πάρα.

ΠΕΝΘΕΥΣ
    στείχοιμ' ἄν· ἢ γὰρ ὅπλ' ἔχων πορεύσομαι   845
    ἢ τοῖσι σοῖσι πείσομαι βουλεύμασιν.

ΔΙΟΝΥΣΟΣ
    γυναῖκες, ἁνὴρ ἐς βόλον καθίσταται,
    ἥξει δὲ βάκχας, οὗ θανὼν δώσει δίκην.
    Διόνυσε, νῦν σὸν ἔργον· οὐ γὰρ εἶ πρόσω·
    τεισώμεθ' αὐτόν. πρῶτα δ' ἔκστησον φρενῶν,   850
    ἐνεὶς ἐλαφρὰν λύσσαν· ὡς φρονῶν μὲν εὖ
    οὐ μὴ θελήσῃ θῆλυν ἐνδῦναι στολήν,
    ἔξω δ' ἐλαύνων τοῦ φρονεῖν ἐνδύσεται.
    χρῄζω δέ νιν γέλωτα Θηβαίοις ὀφλεῖν
    γυναικόμορφον ἀγόμενον δι' ἄστεως   855
    ἐκ τῶν ἀπειλῶν τῶν πρίν, αἷσι δεινὸς ἦν.
    ἀλλ' εἶμι κόσμον ὅνπερ εἰς Ἅιδου λαβὼν
    ἄπεισι μητρὸς ἐκ χεροῖν κατασφαγείς,
    Πενθεῖ προσάψων· γνώσεται δὲ τὸν Διὸς
    Διόνυσον, ὃς πέφυκεν ἐν τέλει θεός,   860
    δεινότατος, ἀνθρώποισι δ' ἠπιώτατος.

ΧΟΡΟΣ
    ἆρ' ἐν παννυχίοις χοροῖς
    θήσω ποτὲ λευκὸν
    πόδ' ἀναβακχεύουσα, δέραν
    εἰς αἰθέρα δροσερὸν ῥίπτουσ',   865

72

DIONYSUS

> We go by deserted streets. I'll take you.

PENTHEUS

> Well, anything is easier to accept
> than being made a fool by Bacchic women.
> Let's go into the house. I'll think about what's best.

DIONYSUS

> As you wish. Whatever you do, I'm ready.

PENTHEUS

> I think I'll go in now. It's a choice
> of going with weapons or taking your advice.

[Exit Pentheus into the palace. Dionysus turns to face the chorus]

DIONYSUS

> My women! that man's now entangled in our net.
> He'll go to those Bacchae, and there he'll die.
> That will be his punishment. Dionysus,
> you're not far away. Now it's up to you.
> Punish him. First, make sure he goes insane   [850]
> with some crazed fantasy. If his mind is strong,
> he'll not agree to put on women's clothes.
> But he'll do it, if you make him mad.
> I want him made the laughing stock of Thebes,
> while I lead him through the city, mincing
> as he moves along in women's clothing,
> after he made himself so terrifying
> with all those earlier threats. Now I'll be off,
> to fit Pentheus into the costume
> he'll wear when he goes down to Hades,
> once he's butchered by his mother's hands.
> He'll come to acknowledge Dionysus,
> son of Zeus, born in full divinity,   [860]
> most fearful and yet most kind to men.

[Exit Dionysus]

CHORUS

> O when will I be dancing,
>   leaping barefoot through the night,
> flinging back my head in ecstasy,
> in the clear, cold, dew-fresh air —

73

ὡς νεβρὸς χλοεραῖς ἐμπαί-
ζουσα λείμακος ἡδοναῖς,
ἡνίκ᾽ ἂν φοβερὰν φύγῃ
θήραν ἔξω φυλακᾶς
εὐπλέκτων ὑπὲρ ἀρκύων,   870
θωύσσων δὲ κυναγέτας
συντείνῃ δράμημα κυνῶν·
μόχθοις τ᾽ ὠκυδρόμοις τ᾽ ἀέλ-
λαις θρῴσκει πεδίον
παραποτάμιον, ἡδομένα   875
βροτῶν ἐρημίαις σκιαρο-
κόμοιό τ᾽ ἔρνεσιν ὕλας.

τί τὸ σοφόν; ἢ τί τὸ κάλλιον
παρὰ θεῶν γέρας ἐν βροτοῖς
ἢ χεῖρ᾽ ὑπὲρ κορυφᾶς
τῶν ἐχθρῶν κρείσσω κατέχειν;   880
ὅ τι καλὸν φίλον ἀεί.

ὁρμᾶται μόλις, ἀλλ᾽ ὅμως
πιστόν τι τὸ θεῖον
σθένος· ἀπευθύνει δὲ βροτῶν
τούς τ᾽ ἀγνωμοσύναν τιμῶν-   885
τας καὶ μὴ τὰ θεῶν αὔξον-
τας σὺν μαινομένᾳ δόξᾳ.
κρυπτεύουσι δὲ ποικίλως
δαρὸν χρόνου πόδα καὶ
θηρῶσιν τὸν ἄσεπτον. οὐ   890
γὰρ κρεῖσσόν ποτε τῶν νόμων
γιγνώσκειν χρὴ καὶ μελετᾶν.
κούφα γὰρ δαπάνα νομί-
ζειν ἰσχὺν τόδ᾽ ἔχειν,
ὅ τι ποτ᾽ ἄρα τὸ δαιμόνιον,
τό τ᾽ ἐν χρόνῳ μακρῷ νόμιμον   895
ἀεὶ φύσει τε πεφυκός.

τί τὸ σοφόν; ἢ τί τὸ κάλλιον
παρὰ θεῶν γέρας ἐν βροτοῖς

74

like a playful fawn
celebrating its green joy
across the meadows —
joy that it's escaped the fearful hunt —
as she runs beyond the hunters,
leaping past their woven nets — [870]
they call out to their hounds
to chase her with still more speed,
but she strains every limb,
racing like a wind storm,
rejoicing by the river plain,
in places where no hunters lurk,
in the green living world
beneath the shady branches,
the foliage of the trees.

What is wisdom? What is finer
than the rights men get from gods —
to hold their powerful hands
over the heads of their enemies? [880]
Ah yes, what's good is always loved.

The power of the gods
is difficult to stir —
but it's a power we can count on.
It punishes all mortal men
who honour their own ruthless wills,
who, in their fits of madness,
fail to reverence the gods.
Gods track down every man
who scorns their worship,
using their cunning to conceal
the enduring steady pace of time. [890]
For there's no righteousness
in those who recognize or practice
what's beyond our customary laws.
The truth is easy to acknowledge:
whatever is divine is mighty,
whatever has been long-established law
is an eternal natural truth.

What is wisdom? What is finer
than the rights men get from gods —

75

ἢ χεῖρ' ὑπὲρ κορυφᾶς
τῶν ἐχθρῶν κρείσσω κατέχειν;　　　　　　900
ὅ τι καλὸν φίλον ἀεί.

εὐδαίμων μὲν ὃς ἐκ θαλάσσας
ἔφυγε χεῖμα, λιμένα δ' ἔκιχεν·
εὐδαίμων δ' ὃς ὕπερθε μόχθων
ἐγένεθ'· ἑτέρα δ' ἕτερος ἕτερον　　　　　905
ὄλβῳ καὶ δυνάμει παρῆλθεν.
μυρίαι δ' ἔτι μυρίοις
εἰσὶν ἐλπίδες· αἲ μὲν
τελευτῶσιν ἐν ὄλβῳ
βροτοῖς, αἲ δ' ἀπέβησαν·
τὸ δὲ κατ' ἦμαρ ὅτῳ βίοτος　　　　　　910
εὐδαίμων, μακαρίζω.

ΔΙΟΝΥΣΟΣ

σὲ τὸν πρόθυμον ὄνθ' ἃ μὴ χρεὼν ὁρᾶν
σπεύδοντά τ' ἀσπούδαστα, Πενθέα λέγω,
ἔξιθι πάροιθε δωμάτων, ὄφθητί μοι,
σκευὴν γυναικὸς μαινάδος βάκχης ἔχων,　　915
μητρός τε τῆς σῆς καὶ λόχου κατάσκοπος·
πρέπεις δὲ Κάδμου θυγατέρων μορφὴν μιᾷ.

ΠΕΝΘΕΥΣ

καὶ μὴν ὁρᾶν μοι δύο μὲν ἡλίους δοκῶ,
δισσὰς δὲ Θήβας καὶ πόλισμ' ἑπτάστομον·
καὶ ταῦρος ἡμῖν πρόσθεν ἡγεῖσθαι δοκεῖς　　920
καὶ σῷ κέρατα κρατὶ προσπεφυκέναι.
ἀλλ' ἦ ποτ' ἦσθα θήρ; τεταύρωσαι γὰρ οὖν.

to hold their powerful hands
over the heads of their enemies? [900]
Ah yes, what's good is always loved.

Whoever has escaped a storm at sea
is a happy man in harbour,
whoever overcomes great hardship
is likewise another happy man.
Various men out-do each other
in wealth, in power,
in all sorts of ways.
The hopes of countless men
are infinite in number.
Some make men rich;
some come to nothing.
So I consider that man blessed
who lives a happy life [910]
existing day by day.

[Enter Dionysus from the palace. He calls back through the open doors]

DIONYSUS
You who are so desperately eager
to see those things you should not look upon,
so keen to chase what you should not pursue—
I mean you, Pentheus, come out here now,
outside the palace, where I can see you
dressed up as a raving Bacchic female,
to spy upon your mother's company.

[Enter Pentheus dressed in women's clothing. He moves in a deliberately over-stated female way, enjoying the role]

DIONYSUS *[admiringly, as he escorts Pentheus from the doors]*
You look just like one of Cadmus' daughters.

PENTHEUS
Fancy that! I seem to see two suns,
two images of seven-gated Thebes.
And you look like a bull leading me out here, [920]
with those horns growing from your head.
Were you once upon a time a beast?
It's certain now you've changed into a bull.

ΔΙΟΝΥΣΟΣ

ὁ θεὸς ὁμαρτεῖ, πρόσθεν ὢν οὐκ εὐμενής,
ἔνσπονδος ἡμῖν· νῦν δ᾽ ὁρᾷς ἃ χρή σ᾽ ὁρᾶν.

ΠΕΝΘΕΥΣ

τί φαίνομαι δῆτ᾽; οὐχὶ τὴν Ἰνοῦς στάσιν   925
ἢ τὴν Ἀγαύης ἑστάναι, μητρός γ᾽ ἐμῆς;

ΔΙΟΝΥΣΟΣ

αὐτὰς ἐκείνας εἰσορᾶν δοκῶ σ᾽ ὁρῶν.
ἀλλ᾽ ἐξ ἕδρας σοι πλόκαμος ἐξέστηχ᾽ ὅδε,
οὐχ ὡς ἐγώ νιν ὑπὸ μίτρᾳ καθήρμοσα.

ΠΕΝΘΕΥΣ

ἔνδον προσείων αὐτὸν ἀνασείων τ᾽ ἐγὼ   930
καὶ βακχιάζων ἐξ ἕδρας μεθώρμισα.

ΔΙΟΝΥΣΟΣ

ἀλλ᾽ αὐτὸν ἡμεῖς, οἷς σε θεραπεύειν μέλει,
πάλιν καταστελοῦμεν· ἀλλ᾽ ὄρθου κάρα.

ΠΕΝΘΕΥΣ

ἰδού, σὺ κόσμει· σοὶ γὰρ ἀνακείμεσθα δή.

ΔΙΟΝΥΣΟΣ

ζῶναί τέ σοι χαλῶσι κοὐχ ἑξῆς πέπλων   935
στολίδες ὑπὸ σφυροῖσι τείνουσιν σέθεν.

ΠΕΝΘΕΥΣ

κἀμοὶ δοκοῦσι παρά γε δεξιὸν πόδα·
τἀνθένδε δ᾽ ὀρθῶς παρὰ τένοντ᾽ ἔχει πέπλος.

ΔΙΟΝΥΣΟΣ

ἦ πού με τῶν σῶν πρῶτον ἡγήσῃ φίλων,
ὅταν παρὰ λόγον σώφρονας βάκχας ἴδῃς.   940

DIONYSUS

>The god walks here. He's made a pact with us.
>Before his attitude was not so kind.
>Now you're seeing just what you ought to see.

PENTHEUS

>How do I look? Am I holding myself
>just like Ino or my mother, Agave?

DIONYSUS

>When I look at you, I think I see them.
>But here, this strand of hair is out of place.
>It's not under the headband where I fixed it.

PENTHEUS *[demonstrating his dancing steps]*

>I must have worked it loose inside the house,   [930]
>shaking my head when I moved here and there,
>practising my Bacchanalian dance.

DIONYSUS

>I'll rearrange it for you. It's only right
>that I should serve you. Straighten up your head.

[Dionysus begins adjusting Pentheus' hair and clothing]

PENTHEUS

>All right then. You can be my dresser,
>now that I've transformed myself for you.

DIONYSUS

>Your girdle's loose. And these pleats in your dress
>are crooked, too, down at your ankle here.

PENTHEUS *[examining the back of his legs]*

>Yes, that seems to be true for my right leg,
>but on this side the dress hangs perfectly,
>down the full length of my limb.

DIONYSUS

>   Once you see
>those Bacchic women acting modestly,
>once you confront something you don't expect,   [940]
>you'll consider me your dearest friend.

79

ΠΕΝΘΕΥΣ

πότερα δὲ θύρσον δεξιᾷ λαβὼν χερὶ
ἢ τῇδε, βάκχῃ μᾶλλον εἰκασθήσομαι;

ΔΙΟΝΥΣΟΣ

ἐν δεξιᾷ χρὴ χἅμα δεξιῷ ποδὶ
αἴρειν νιν· αἰνῶ δ' ὅτι μεθέστηκας φρενῶν.

ΠΕΝΘΕΥΣ

ἆρ' ἂν δυναίμην τὰς Κιθαιρῶνος πτυχὰς   945
αὐταῖσι βάκχαις τοῖς ἐμοῖς ὤμοις φέρειν;

ΔΙΟΝΥΣΟΣ

δύναι' ἄν, εἰ βούλοιο· τὰς δὲ πρὶν φρένας
οὐκ εἶχες ὑγιεῖς, νῦν δ' ἔχεις οἵας σε δεῖ.

ΠΕΝΘΕΥΣ

μοχλοὺς φέρωμεν; ἢ χεροῖν ἀνασπάσω
κορυφαῖς ὑποβαλὼν ὦμον ἢ βραχίονα;   950

ΔΙΟΝΥΣΟΣ

μὴ σύ γε τὰ Νυμφῶν διολέσῃς ἱδρύματα
καὶ Πανὸς ἕδρας ἔνθ' ἔχει συρίγματα.

ΠΕΝΘΕΥΣ

καλῶς ἔλεξας· οὐ σθένει νικητέον
γυναῖκας· ἐλάταισιν δ' ἐμὸν κρύψω δέμας.

ΔΙΟΝΥΣΟΣ

κρύψῃ σὺ κρύψιν ἥν σε κρυφθῆναι χρεών,   955
ἐλθόντα δόλιον μαινάδων κατάσκοπον.

ΠΕΝΘΕΥΣ

καὶ μὴν δοκῶ σφᾶς ἐν λόχμαις ὄρνιθας ὣς
λέκτρων ἔχεσθαι φιλτάτοις ἐν ἕρκεσιν.

PENTHEUS

This thyrsus — should I hold it in my right hand,
or in my left? Which is more suitable
in Bacchic celebrations?

DIONYSUS

In your right.
You must lift your right foot in time with it.

[Dionysus observes Pentheus trying out the dance step]

DIONYSUS

Your mind has changed. I applaud you for it.

PENTHEUS

Will I be powerful enough to carry
the forests of Cithaeron on my shoulders,
along with all those Bacchic females?

DIONYSUS

If you have desire, you'll have the power.
Before this your mind was not well adjusted.
But now it's working in you as it should.

PENTHEUS

Are we going to take some levers with us?
Or shall I rip the forests up by hand,
putting arm and shoulder under mountain peaks?   [950]

DIONYSUS

As long as you don't do away with
those places where the nymphs all congregate,
where Pan plays his music on his pipes.

PENTHEUS

You mention a good point. I'll use no force
to get the better of these women.
I'll conceal myself there in the pine trees.

DIONYSUS

You'll find just the sort of hiding place
a spy should find who wants to hide himself,
so he can gaze upon the Maenads.

PENTHEUS

That's good. I can picture them right now,
in the woods, going at it like rutting birds,
clutching each other as they make sweet love.

81

ΔΙΟΝΥΣΟΣ

οὐκοῦν ἐπ᾽ αὐτὸ τοῦτ᾽ ἀποστέλλῃ φύλαξ·
λήψῃ δ᾽ ἴσως σφᾶς, ἢν σὺ μὴ ληφθῇς πάρος.　　　960

ΠΕΝΘΕΥΣ

κόμιζε διὰ μέσης με Θηβαίας χθονός·
μόνος γὰρ αὐτῶν εἰμ᾽ ἀνὴρ τολμῶν τόδε.

ΔΙΟΝΥΣΟΣ

μόνος σὺ πόλεως τῆσδ᾽ ὑπερκάμνεις, μόνος·
τοιγάρ σ᾽ ἀγῶνες ἀναμένουσιν οὓς ἐχρῆν.
ἕπου δέ· πομπὸς δ᾽ εἶμ᾽ ἐγὼ σωτήριος,　　　965
κεῖθεν δ᾽ ἀπάξει σ᾽ ἄλλος.

ΠΕΝΘΕΥΣ

　　　　　　　ἡ τεκοῦσά γε.

ΔΙΟΝΥΣΟΣ

ἐπίσημον ὄντα πᾶσιν.

ΠΕΝΘΕΥΣ

　　　　　　　ἐπὶ τόδ᾽ ἔρχομαι.

ΔΙΟΝΥΣΟΣ

φερόμενος ἥξεις . . .

ΠΕΝΘΕΥΣ

　　　　　　　ἁβρότητ᾽ ἐμὴν λέγεις.

ΔΙΟΝΥΣΟΣ

ἐν χερσὶ μητρός.

ΠΕΝΘΕΥΣ

　　　　　　　καὶ τρυφᾶν μ᾽ ἀναγκάσεις.

ΔΙΟΝΥΣΟΣ

τρυφάς γε τοιάσδε.　　　970

ΠΕΝΘΕΥΣ

　　　　　　　ἀξίων μὲν ἅπτομαι.

DIONYSUS

Perhaps. That's why you're going—as a guard
to stop all that. Maybe you'll capture them,   [960]
unless you're captured first.

PENTHEUS

Lead on—
through the centre of our land of Thebes.
I'm the only man in all the city
who dares to undertake this enterprise.

DIONYSUS

You bear the city's burden by yourself,
all by yourself. So your work is waiting there,
the tasks that have been specially set for you.
Follow me. I'm the guide who'll rescue you.
When you return someone else will bring you back.

PENTHEUS

That will be my mother.

DIONYSUS

For everyone
you'll have become someone to celebrate.

PENTHEUS

That's why I'm going.

DIONYSUS

You'll be carried back . . .

PENTHEUS: *[interrupting]*

You're pampering me!

DIONYSUS *[continuing]*

. . . in your mother's arms.

PENTHEUS

You've really made up your mind to spoil me.

DIONYSUS

To spoil you? That's true, but in my own way.

PENTHEUS

Then I'll be off to get what I deserve.   [970]

[Exit Pentheus]

83

ΔΙΟΝΥΣΟΣ

δεινὸς σὺ δεινὸς κἀπὶ δείν᾽ ἔρχῃ πάθη,
ὥστ᾽ οὐρανῷ στηρίζον εὑρήσεις κλέος.
ἔκτειν᾽, Ἀγαύη, χεῖρας αἵ θ᾽ ὁμόσποροι
Κάδμου θυγατέρες· τὸν νεανίαν ἄγω
τόνδ᾽ εἰς ἀγῶνα μέγαν, ὁ νικήσων δ᾽ ἐγὼ   975
καὶ Βρόμιος ἔσται. τἄλλα δ᾽ αὐτὸ σημανεῖ.

ΧΟΡΟΣ

ἴτε θοαὶ Λύσσας κύνες ἴτ᾽ εἰς ὄρος,
θίασον ἔνθ᾽ ἔχουσι Κάδμου κόραι,
ἀνοιστρήσατέ νιν
ἐπὶ τὸν ἐν γυναικομίμῳ στολᾷ   980
λυσσώδη κατάσκοπον μαινάδων.
μάτηρ πρῶτά νιν λευρᾶς ἀπὸ πέτρας
ἢ σκόλοπος ὄψεται
δοκεύοντα, μαινάσιν δ᾽ ἀπύσει·
Τίς ὅδ᾽ ὀρειδρόμων   985
μαστὴρ Καδμείων ἐς ὄρος ἐς ὄρος ἔμολ᾽
ἔμολεν, ὦ βάκχαι; τίς ἄρα νιν ἔτεκεν;
οὐ γὰρ ἐξ αἵματος
γυναικῶν ἔφυ, λεαίνας δέ τινος
ὅδ᾽ ἢ Γοργόνων Λιβυσσᾶν γένος.   990

— ἴτω δίκα φανερός, ἴτω ξιφηφόρος   992
φονεύουσα λαιμῶν διαμπὰξ
τὸν ἄθεον ἄνομον ἄδικον Ἐχίονος   995
γόνον γηγενῆ.

84

DIONYSUS *[speaking in the direction Pentheus has gone, but not speaking to him]*
>You fearful, terrifying man — on your way
>to horrific suffering. Well, you'll win
>a towering fame, as high as heaven.
>Hold out your hand to him, Agave,
>you, too, her sisters, Cadmus' daughters.
>I'm leading this young man in your direction,
>for the great confrontation, where I'll triumph —
>I and Bromius. What else will happen
>events will show, as they occur.

[Exit Dionysus]

CHORUS 1
>Up now, you hounds of madness,
>go up now into the mountains,
>go where Cadmus' daughters
>keep their company of worshippers,   [980]
>goad them into furious revenge
>against that man, that raving spy,
>all dressed up in his women's clothes,
>so keen to glimpse the Maenads.
>His mother will see him first,
>as he spies on them in secret
>from some level rock or crag.
>She'll scream out to her Maenads,
>"Who's the man who's come here,
>to the mountains, to these mountains,
>tracking Cadmean mountain dancers?
>O my Bacchae, who has come?
>From whom was this man born?
>He's not born of woman's blood —
>he must be some lioness' whelp
>or spawned from Libyan gorgons."   [990]

CHORUS
>Let justice manifest itself —
>let justice march, sword in hand,
>to stab him in the throat,
>that godless, lawless man,
>unjust earthborn seed of Echion.

— ὃς ἀδίκῳ γνώμᾳ παρανόμῳ τ᾽ ὀργᾷ
περὶ σὰ Βάκχι᾽, ὄργια ματρός τε σᾶς
μανείσᾳ πραπίδι
παρακόπῳ τε λήματι στέλλεται,   1000
τἀνίκατον ὡς κρατήσων βίᾳ,
γνωμᾶν σωφρόνα θάνατος ἀπροφάσι-
στος ἐς τὰ θεῶν ἔφυ·
βροτείως τ᾽ ἔχειν ἄλυπος βίος.
τὸ σοφὸν οὐ φθονῶ·   1005
χαίρω θηρεύουσα· τὰ δ᾽ ἕτερα μεγάλα
φανερά τ᾽· ὤ, νάειν ἐπὶ τὰ καλὰ βίον,
ἦμαρ ἐς νύκτα τ᾽ εὐ-
αγοῦντ᾽ εὐσεβεῖν, τὰ δ᾽ ἔξω νόμιμα
δίκας ἐκβαλόντα τιμᾶν θεούς.   1010

— ἴτω δίκα φανερός, ἴτω ξιφηφόρος   1013
φονεύουσα λαιμῶν διαμπὰξ
τὸν ἄθεον ἄνομον ἄδικον Ἐχίονος   1015
τόκον γηγενῆ.

— φάνηθι ταῦρος ἢ πολύκρανος ἰδεῖν   1018
δράκων ἢ πυριφλέγων ὁρᾶσθαι λέων.
ἴθ᾽, ὦ Βάκχε, θηραγρευτᾷ βακχᾶν   1020
γελῶντι προσώπῳ περίβαλε βρόχον
θανάσιμον ὑπ᾽ ἀγέλαν πεσόν-
τι τὰν μαινάδων.

ἌΓΓΕΛΟΣ Β
    ὦ δῶμ᾽ ὃ πρίν ποτ᾽ εὐτύχεις ἀν᾽ Ἑλλάδα,
    Σιδωνίου γέροντος, ὃς τὸ γηγενὲς   1025

CHORUS 2

> Any man intent on wickedness,
> turning his unlawful rage
> against your rites, O Bacchus,
> against the worship of your mother,
> a man who sets out with an insane mind,   [1000]
> his courage founded on a falsehood,
> who seeks to overcome by force
> what simply can't be overcome—
> let death set his intentions straight.
> For a life devoid of grief is one
> which receives without complaint
> whatever comes down from the gods—
> that's how mortals ought to live.
> Wisdom is something I don't envy.
> My joy comes hunting other things
> lofty and plain to everyone.
> They lead man's life to good
> in purity and reverence,
> honouring gods day and night,
> eradicating from our lives
> customs lying beyond what's right.   [1010]

CHORUS

> Let justice manifest itself—
> Let justice march, sword in hand,
> to stab him in the throat,
> that godless, lawless man,
> unjust earthborn seed of Echion.

CHORUS 3

> Appear now to our sight, O Bacchus—
> come as a bull or many-headed serpent
> or else some fire-breathing lion.
> Go now, Bacchus, with your smiling face   [1020]
> cast your deadly noose upon
> that hunter of the Bacchae,
> as the group of Maenads brings him down.

[Enter Second Messenger, one of Pentheus' attendants]

SECOND MESSENGER

> How I grieve for this house, in earlier days
> so happy throughout Greece, home of that old man,

δράκοντος ἔσπειρ᾽ Ὄφεος ἐν γαίᾳ θέρος,
ὥς σε στενάζω, δοῦλος ὢν μέν, ἀλλ᾽ ὅμως
χρηστοῖσι δούλοις συμφορὰ τὰ δεσποτῶν.

ΧΟΡΟΣ

τί δ᾽ ἔστιν; ἐκ βακχῶν τι μηνύεις νέον;

ΆΓΓΕΛΟΣ

Πενθεὺς ὄλωλεν, παῖς Ἐχίονος πατρός.   1030

ΧΟΡΟΣ

ὦναξ Βρόμιε, θεὸς φαίνῃ μέγας.

ΆΓΓΕΛΟΣ

πῶς φῄς; τί τοῦτ᾽ ἔλεξας; ἦ 'πὶ τοῖς ἐμοῖς
χαίρεις κακῶς πράσσουσι δεσπόταις, γύναι;

ΧΟΡΟΣ

εὐάζω ξένα μέλεσι βαρβάροις·
οὐκέτι γὰρ δεσμῶν ὑπὸ φόβῳ πτήσσω.   1035

ΆΓΓΕΛΟΣ

Θήβας δ᾽ ἀνάνδρους ὧδ᾽ ἄγεις . . .

ΧΟΡΟΣ

ὁ Διόνυσος ὁ Διόνυσος, οὐ Θῆβαι
κράτος ἔχουσ᾽ ἐμόν.

ΆΓΓΕΛΟΣ

συγγνωστὰ μέν σοι, πλὴν ἐπ᾽ ἐξειργασμένοις
κακοῖσι χαίρειν, ὦ γυναῖκες, οὐ καλόν.   1040

Cadmus from Sidon, who sowed the fields
to harvest the earth-born crop produced
from serpent Ophis. How I now lament—
I know I'm just a slave, but nonetheless . . .

CHORUS

Do you bring us news?
Has something happened,
something about the Bacchae?

SECOND MESSENGER

Pentheus, child of Echion, is dead.   [1030]

CHORUS

O my lord Bromius,
Now your divine greatness
is here made manifest!

SECOND MESSENGER

What are you saying? Why that song?
Women, how can you now rejoice like this
for the death of one who was my master?

CHORUS LEADER

We're strangers here in Thebes,
so we sing out our joy
in chants from foreign lands.
No longer need we cower here
in fear of prisoner's chains.

SECOND MESSENGER

Do you think Thebes lacks sufficient men
to take care of your punishment?

CHORUS

Dionysus, oh Dionysus,
he's the one with power over me—
not Thebes.

SECOND MESSENGER

That you may be forgiven, but to cry
aloud with joy when such disasters come,
women, that's not something you should so.   [1040]

ΧΟΡΟΣ
ἔννεπέ μοι, φράσον, τίνι μόρῳ θνῄσκει
ἄδικος ἄδικά τ᾿ ἐκπορίζων ἀνήρ;

ἌΓΓΕΛΟΣ
ἐπεὶ θεράπνας τῆσδε Θηβαίας χθονὸς
λιπόντες ἐξέβημεν Ἀσωποῦ ῥοάς,
λέπας Κιθαιρώνειον εἰσεβάλλομεν   1045
Πενθεύς τε κἀγώ—δεσπότῃ γὰρ εἱπόμην—
ξένος θ᾿ ὃς ἡμῖν πομπὸς ἦν θεωρίας.
πρῶτον μὲν οὖν ποιηρὸν ἵζομεν νάπος,
τά τ᾿ ἐκ ποδῶν σιγηλὰ καὶ γλώσσης ἄπο
σῴζοντες, ὡς ὁρῷμεν οὐχ ὁρώμενοι.   1050
ἦν δ᾿ ἄγκος ἀμφίκρημνον, ὕδασι διάβροχον,
πεύκαισι συσκιάζον, ἔνθα μαινάδες
καθῆντ᾿ ἔχουσαι χεῖρας ἐν τερπνοῖς πόνοις.
αἳ μὲν γὰρ αὐτῶν θύρσον ἐκλελοιπότα
κισσῷ κομήτην αὖθις ἐξανέστεφον,   1055
αἳ δ᾿, ἐκλιποῦσαι ποικίλ᾿ ὡς πῶλοι ζυγά,
βακχεῖον ἀντέκλαζον ἀλλήλαις μέλος.
Πενθεὺς δ᾿ ὁ τλήμων θῆλυν οὐχ ὁρῶν ὄχλον
ἔλεξε τοιάδ᾿· Ὦ ξέν᾿, οὗ μὲν ἕσταμεν,
οὐκ ἐξικνοῦμαι μαινάδων ὄσσοις νόθων·   1060
ὄχθων δ᾿ ἔπ᾿, ἀμβὰς ἐς ἐλάτην ὑψαύχενα,
ἴδοιμ᾿ ἂν ὀρθῶς μαινάδων αἰσχρουργίαν.
τοὐντεῦθεν ἤδη τοῦ ξένου τὸ θαῦμ᾿ ὁρῶ·
λαβὼν γὰρ ἐλάτης οὐράνιον ἄκρον κλάδον
κατῆγεν, ἦγεν, ἦγεν ἐς μέλαν πέδον·   1065
κυκλοῦτο δ᾿ ὥστε τόξον ἢ κυρτὸς τροχὸς
τόρνῳ γραφόμενος περιφορὰν ἕλκει δρόμον·
ὣς κλῶν᾿ ὄρειον ὁ ξένος χεροῖν ἄγων
ἔκαμπτεν ἐς γῆν, ἔργματ᾿ οὐχὶ θνητὰ δρῶν.
Πενθέα δ᾿ ἱδρύσας ἐλατίνων ὄζων ἔπι,   1070
ὀρθὸν μεθίει διὰ χερῶν βλάστημ᾿ ἄνω

CHORUS

Speak to me, tell all —
How did death strike him down,
that unrighteous man,
that man who acted so unjustly?

SECOND MESSENGER

Once we'd left the settlements of Thebes,
we went across the river Asopus,
then started the climb up Mount Cithaeron —
Pentheus and myself, I following the king.
The stranger was our guide, scouting the way.
First, we sat down in a grassy meadow,
keeping our feet and tongues quite silent,
so we could see without being noticed.   [1050]
There was a valley there shut in by cliffs.
Through it refreshing waters flowed, with pines
providing shade. The Maenads sat there,
their hands all busy with delightful work —
some of them with ivy strands repairing
damaged thyrsoi, while others sang,
chanting Bacchic songs to one another,
carefree as fillies freed from harness.
Then Pentheus, that unhappy man,
not seeing the crowd of women, spoke up,
"Stranger, I can't see from where we're standing.
My eyes can't glimpse those crafty Maenads.   [1060]
But up there, on that hill, a pine tree stands.
If I climbed that, I might see those women,
and witness the disgraceful things they do."
Then I saw that stranger work a marvel.
He seized that pine tree's topmost branch —
it stretched up to heaven — and brought it down,
pulling it to the dark earth, bending it
as if it were a bow or some curved wheel
forced into a circle while staked out with pegs —
that's how the stranger made that tree bend down,
forcing the mountain pine to earth by hand,
something no mortal man could ever do.
He set Pentheus in that pine tree's branches.   [1070]
Then his hands released the tree, but slowly,
so it stood up straight, being very careful

91

ἀτρέμα, φυλάσσων μὴ ἀναχαιτίσειέ νιν,
ὀρθὴ δ᾽ ἐς ὀρθὸν αἰθέρ᾽ ἐστηρίζετο,
ἔχουσα νώτοις δεσπότην ἐφήμενον·
ὤφθη δὲ μᾶλλον ἢ κατεῖδε μαινάδας.   1075
ὅσον γὰρ οὔπω δῆλος ἦν θάσσων ἄνω,
καὶ τὸν ξένον μὲν οὐκέτ᾽ εἰσορᾶν παρῆν,
ἐκ δ᾽ αἰθέρος φωνή τις, ὡς μὲν εἰκάσαι
Διόνυσος, ἀνεβόησεν· Ὦ νεάνιδες,
ἄγω τὸν ὑμᾶς κἀμὲ τἀμά τ᾽ ὄργια   1080
γέλων τιθέμενον· ἀλλὰ τιμωρεῖσθέ νιν.
καὶ ταῦθ᾽ ἅμ᾽ ἠγόρευε καὶ πρὸς οὐρανὸν
καὶ γαῖαν ἐστήριξε φῶς σεμνοῦ πυρός.
σίγησε δ᾽ αἰθήρ, σῖγα δ᾽ ὕλιμος νάπη
φύλλ᾽ εἶχε, θηρῶν δ᾽ οὐκ ἂν ἤκουσας βοήν.   1085
αἱ δ᾽ ὠσὶν ἠχὴν οὐ σαφῶς δεδεγμέναι
ἔστησαν ὀρθαὶ καὶ διήνεγκαν κόρας.
ὁ δ᾽ αὖθις ἐπεκέλευσεν· ὡς δ᾽ ἐγνώρισαν
σαφῆ κελευσμὸν Βακχίου Κάδμου κόραι,
ᾖξαν πελείας ὠκύτητ᾽ οὐχ ἥσσονες   1090
ποδῶν τρέχουσαι συντόνοις δραμήμασι,
μήτηρ Ἀγαύη σύγγονοί θ᾽ ὁμόσποροι
πᾶσαί τε βάκχαι· διὰ δὲ χειμάρρου νάπης
ἀγμῶν τ᾽ ἐπήδων θεοῦ πνοαῖσιν ἐμμανεῖς.
ὡς δ᾽ εἶδον ἐλάτῃ δεσπότην ἐφήμενον,   1095
πρῶτον μὲν αὐτοῦ χερμάδας κραταιβόλους
ἔρριπτον, ἀντίπυργον ἐπιβᾶσαι πέτραν,
ὄζοισί τ᾽ ἐλατίνοισιν ἠκοντίζετο.
ἄλλαι δὲ θύρσους ἵεσαν δι᾽ αἰθέρος
Πενθέως, στόχον δύστηνον· ἀλλ᾽ οὐκ ἤνυτον.   1100
κρεῖσσον γὰρ ὕψος τῆς προθυμίας ἔχων
καθῆσθ᾽ ὁ τλήμων, ἀπορίᾳ λελημμένος.
τέλος δὲ δρυΐνους συγκεραυνοῦσαι κλάδους
ῥίζας ἀνεσπάρασσον ἀσιδήροις μοχλοῖς.
ἐπεὶ δὲ μόχθων τέρματ᾽ οὐκ ἐξήνυτον,   1105
ἔλεξ᾽ Ἀγαύη· Φέρε, περιστᾶσαι κύκλῳ
πτόρθου λάβεσθε, μαινάδες, τὸν ἀμβάτην

not to shake Pentheus loose. So that pine
towered straight up to heaven, with my king
perched on its back. Maenads could see him there
more easily than he could spy on them.
As he was just becoming visible —
the stranger had completely disappeared —
some voice — I guess it was Dionysus —
cried out from the sky, "Young women,
I've brought you the man who laughed at you,   [1080]
who ridiculed my rites. Now punish him!"
As he shouted this, a dreadful fire arose,
blazing between the earth and heaven.
The air was still. In the wooded valley
no sound came from the leaves, and all the beasts
were silent, too. The women stood up at once.
They'd heard the voice, but not distinctly.
They gazed around them. Then again the voice
shouted his commands. When Cadmus' daughters
clearly heard what Dionysus ordered,
they rushed out, running as fast as doves,   [1090]
moving their feet at an amazing speed.
His mother Agave with both her sisters
and all the Bacchae charged straight through
the valley, the torrents, the mountain cliffs,
pushed to a god-inspired frenzy.
They saw the king there sitting in that pine.
First, they scaled a cliff face looming up
opposite the tree and started throwing rocks,
trying to hurt him. Others threw branches,
or hurled their thyrsoi through the air at him,
sad, miserable Pentheus, their target.   [1100]
But they didn't hit him. The poor man
sat high beyond their frenzied cruelty,
trapped up there, no way to save his skin.
Then, like lightning, they struck oak branches down,
trying them as levers to uproot the tree.
When these attempts all failed, Agave said,
"Come now, make a circle round the tree.
Then, Maenads, each of you must seize a branch,

θῆρ' ὡς ἕλωμεν, μηδ' ἀπαγγείλῃ θεοῦ
χοροὺς κρυφαίους. αἳ δὲ μυρίαν χέρα
προσέθεσαν ἐλάτῃ κἀξανέσπασαν χθονός·   1110
ὑψοῦ δὲ θάσσων ὑψόθεν χαμαιριφὴς
πίπτει πρὸς οὖδας μυρίοις οἰμώγμασιν
Πενθεύς· κακοῦ γὰρ ἐγγὺς ὢν ἐμάνθανεν.
πρώτη δὲ μήτηρ ἦρξεν ἱερέα φόνου
καὶ προσπίτνει νιν· ὃ δὲ μίτραν κόμης ἄπο   1115
ἔρριψεν, ὥς νιν γνωρίσασα μὴ κτάνοι
τλήμων Ἀγαύη, καὶ λέγει, παρηῖδος
ψαύων· Ἐγώ τοι, μῆτερ, εἰμί, παῖς σέθεν
Πενθεύς, ὃν ἔτεκες ἐν δόμοις Ἐχίονος·
οἴκτιρε δ' ὦ μῆτέρ με, μηδὲ ταῖς ἐμαῖς   1120
ἁμαρτίαισι παῖδα σὸν κατακτάνῃς.
ἣ δ' ἀφρὸν ἐξιεῖσα καὶ διαστρόφους
κόρας ἑλίσσουσ', οὐ φρονοῦσ' ἃ χρὴ φρονεῖν,
ἐκ Βακχίου κατείχετ', οὐδ' ἔπειθέ νιν.
λαβοῦσα δ' ὠλένης ἀριστερὰν χέρα,   1125
πλευραῖσιν ἀντιβᾶσα τοῦ δυσδαίμονος
ἀπεσπάραξεν ὦμον, οὐχ ὑπὸ σθένους,
ἀλλ' ὁ θεὸς εὐμάρειαν ἐπεδίδου χεροῖν·
Ἰνὼ δὲ τἀπὶ θάτερ' ἐξειργάζετο,
ῥηγνῦσα σάρκας, Αὐτονόη τ' ὄχλος τε πᾶς   1130
ἐπεῖχε βακχῶν· ἦν δὲ πᾶσ' ὁμοῦ βοή,
ὃ μὲν στενάζων ὅσον ἐτύγχαν' ἐμπνέων,
αἳ δ' ἠλάλαζον. ἔφερε δ' ἣ μὲν ὠλένην,
ἣ δ' ἴχνος αὐταῖς ἀρβύλαις· γυμνοῦντο δὲ
πλευραὶ σπαραγμοῖς· πᾶσα δ' ᾑματωμένη   1135
χεῖρας διεσφαίριζε σάρκα Πενθέως.
κεῖται δὲ χωρὶς σῶμα, τὸ μὲν ὑπὸ στύφλοις
πέτραις, τὸ δ' ὕλης ἐν βαθυξύλῳ φόβῃ,
οὐ ῥᾴδιον ζήτημα· κρᾶτα δ' ἄθλιον,
ὅπερ λαβοῦσα τυγχάνει μήτηρ χεροῖν,   1140
πήξασ' ἐπ' ἄκρον θύρσον ὡς ὀρεστέρου

so we can catch the climbing beast up there,
stop him making our god's secret dances known."
Thousands of hands grabbed the tree and pulled.
They yanked it from the ground. Pentheus fell,   [1110]
crashing to earth down from his lofty perch,
screaming in distress. He knew well enough
something dreadful was about to happen.
His priestess mother first began the slaughter.
She hurled herself at him. Pentheus tore off
his headband, untying it from his head,
so wretched Agave would recognize him,
so she wouldn't kill him. Touching her cheek,
he cried out, "It's me, mother, Pentheus,
your child. You gave birth to me at home,
in Echion's house. Pity me, mother—   [1120]
don't kill your child because I've made mistakes."
But Agave was foaming at the mouth,
eyes rolling in their sockets, her mind not set
on what she ought to think—she didn't listen—
she was possessed, in a Bacchic frenzy.
She seized his left arm, below the elbow,
pushed her foot against the poor man's ribs,
then tore his shoulder out. The strength she had—
it was not her own. The god put power
into those hands of hers. Meanwhile Ino,
her sister, went at the other side,
ripping off chunks of Pentheus' flesh,
while Autonoe and all the Bacchae,   [1130]
the whole crowd of them, attacked as well,
all of them howling out together.
As long as Pentheus was still alive,
he kept on screaming. The women cried in triumph—
one brandished an arm, another held a foot—
complete with hunting boot—the women's nails
tore his ribs apart. Their hands grew bloody,
tossing bits of his flesh back and forth, for fun.
His body parts lie scattered everywhere—
some under rough rocks, some in the forest,
deep in the trees. They're difficult to find.
As for the poor victim's head, his mother   [1140]
stumbled on it. Her hands picked it up,
then stuck it on a thyrsus, at the tip.

φέρει λέοντος διὰ Κιθαιρῶνος μέσου,
λιποῦσ᾽ ἀδελφὰς ἐν χοροῖσι μαινάδων.
χωρεῖ δὲ θήρᾳ δυσπότμῳ γαυρουμένη
τειχέων ἔσω τῶνδ᾽, ἀνακαλοῦσα Βάκχιον   1145
τὸν ξυγκύναγον, τὸν ξυνεργάτην ἄγρας,
τὸν καλλίνικον, ᾧ δάκρυα νικηφορεῖ.
ἐγὼ μὲν οὖν τῇδ᾽ ἐκποδὼν τῇ ξυμφορᾷ
ἄπειμ᾽, Ἀγαύην πρὶν μολεῖν πρὸς δώματα.
τὸ σωφρονεῖν δὲ καὶ σέβειν τὰ τῶν θεῶν   1150
κάλλιστον· οἶμαι δ᾽ αὐτὸ καὶ σοφώτατον
θνητοῖσιν εἶναι κτῆμα τοῖσι χρωμένοις.

ΧΟΡΟΣ
ἀναχορεύσωμεν Βάκχιον,
ἀναβοάσωμεν ξυμφορὰν
τὰν τοῦ δράκοντος Πενθέος ἐκγενέτα·   1155
ὃς τὰν θηλυγενῆ στολὰν
νάρθηκά τε, πιστὸν Ἅιδαν,
ἔλαβεν εὔθυρσον,
ταῦρον προηγητῆρα συμφορᾶς ἔχων.
βάκχαι Καδμεῖαι,   1160
τὸν καλλίνικον κλεινὸν ἐξεπράξατε
ἐς στόνον, ἐς δάκρυα.
καλὸς ἀγών, χέρ᾽ αἵματι στάζουσαν
περιβαλεῖν τέκνου.

— ἀλλ᾽, εἰσορῶ γὰρ ἐς δόμους ὁρμωμένην   1165
Πενθέως Ἀγαύην μητέρ᾽ ἐν διαστρόφοις
ὄσσοις, δέχεσθε κῶμον εὐίου θεοῦ.

96

Now she carries it around Cithaeron,
as though it were some wild lion's head.
She's left her sisters dancing with the Maenads.
She's coming here, inside these very walls,
showing off with pride her ill-fated prey,
calling out to her fellow hunter, Bacchus,
her companion in the chase, the winner,
the glorious victor. By serving him,
in her great triumph she wins only tears.
As for me, I'm leaving this disaster,
before Agave gets back home again.
The best thing is to keep one's mind controlled,   [1150]
and worship all that comes down from the gods.
That, in my view, is the wisest custom,
for those who can conduct their lives that way.

[Exit Messenger]

CHORUS

Let's dance to honour Bacchus,
Let's shout to celebrate what's happened here,
happened to Pentheus,
child of the serpent,
who put on women's clothes,
who took up the beautiful and blessed thyrsus—
his certain death,
disaster brought on by the bull.
You Bacchic women   [1160]
descended from old Cadmus,
you've won glorious victory,
one which ends in tears,
which ends in lamentation.
A noble undertaking this,
to drench one's hands in blood,
life blood dripping from one's only son.

CHORUS LEADER

Wait! I see Agave, Pentheus' mother,
on her way home, her eyes transfixed.
Let's now welcome her,
the happy revels of our god of joy!

97

ΆΓΑΥΗ
  Άσιάδες βάκχαι—

ΧΟΡΟΣ
                  τί μ᾽ ὀροθύνεις, ὤ;

ΆΓΑΥΗ
  φέρομεν ἐξ ὀρέων
  ἕλικα νεότομον ἐπὶ μέλαθρα,   1170
  μακάριον θήραν.

ΧΟΡΟΣ
  ὁρῶ καί σε δέξομαι σύγκωμον.

ΆΓΑΥΗ
  ἔμαρψα τόνδ᾽ ἄνευ βρόχων
  λέοντος ἀγροτέρου νέον ἶνιν·
  ὡς ὁρᾶν πάρα.   1175

ΧΟΡΟΣ
  πόθεν ἐρημίας;

ΆΓΑΥΗ
  Κιθαιρὼν . . .

ΧΟΡΟΣ
                  Κιθαιρών;

ΆΓΑΥΗ
  κατεφόνευσέ νιν.

ΧΟΡΟΣ
  τίς ἁ βαλοῦσα;

ΆΓΑΥΗ
                  πρῶτον ἐμὸν τὸ γέρας.
  μάκαιρ᾽ Ἀγαύη κληζόμεθ᾽ ἐν θιάσοις.   1180

ΧΟΡΟΣ
  τίς ἄλλα;

ΆΓΑΥΗ
              τὰ Κάδμου . . .

[Enter Agave, cradling the head of Pentheus]

AGAVE
    Asian Bacchae . . .

CHORUS
                    Why do you appeal to me?

AGAVE *[displaying the head]*
    From the mountains I've brought home   [1170]
    this ivy tendril freshly cut.
    We've had a blessed hunt.

CHORUS
                                I see it.
    As your fellow dancer, I'll accept it.

AGAVE
    I caught this young lion without a trap,
    as you can see.

CHORUS
                    What desert was he in?

AGAVE
    Cithaeron.

CHORUS
                On Cithaeron?

AGAVE
    Cithaeron killed him.

CHORUS
                        Who struck him down?

AGAVE
    The honour of the first blow goes to me.
    In the dancing I'm called blessed Agave.   [1180]

CHORUS
    Who else?

AGAVE
                    Well, from Cadmus . . .

Euripides

ΧΟΡΟΣ
τί Κάδμου;

ἈΓΑΥΗ
γένεθλα
μετ᾽ ἐμὲ μετ᾽ ἐμὲ τοῦδ᾽
ἔθιγε θηρός· εὐτυχής γ᾽ ἅδ᾽ ἄγρα.

ΧΟΡΟΣ
<...>

ἈΓΑΥΗ
μέτεχέ νυν θοίνας.

ΧΟΡΟΣ
τί; μετέχω, τλᾶμον;

ἈΓΑΥΗ
νέος ὁ μόσχος ἄρ-   1185
τι γένυν ὑπὸ κόρυθ᾽ ἁπαλότριχα
κατάκομον θάλλει.

ΧΟΡΟΣ
πρέπει γ᾽ ὥστε θὴρ ἄγραυλος φόβῃ.

ἈΓΑΥΗ
ὁ Βάκχιος κυναγέτας
σοφὸς σοφῶς ἀνέπηλ᾽ ἐπὶ θῆρα   1190
τόνδε μαινάδας.

ΧΟΡΟΣ
ὁ γὰρ ἄναξ ἀγρεύς.

ἈΓΑΥΗ
ἐπαινεῖς;

ΧΟΡΟΣ
ἐπαινῶ.

ἈΓΑΥΗ
τάχα δὲ Καδμεῖοι . . .

CHORUS

From Cadmus what?

AGAVE

His other children laid hands on the beast,
but after me — only after I did first.
We've had good hunting. So come, share our feast.

CHORUS

What? You want me to eat that with you?
Oh you unhappy woman.

AGAVE

This is a young bull. Look at this cheek
It's just growing downy under the crop
of his soft hair.

CHORUS

His hair makes him resemble
some wild beast.

AGAVE

Bacchus is a clever huntsman —   [1190]
he wisely set his Maenads on this beast.

CHORUS

Yes, our master is indeed a hunter.

AGAVE

Have you any praise for me?

CHORUS

I praise you.

AGAVE

Soon all Cadmus' people. . .

ΧΟΡΟΣ
καὶ παῖς γε Πενθεὺς . . .   1195

ΑΓΑΥΗ
                    ματέρ᾽ ἐπαινέσεται,
λαβοῦσαν ἄγραν τάνδε λεοντοφυῆ.

ΧΟΡΟΣ
περισσάν.

ΑΓΑΥΗ
              περισσῶς.

ΧΟΡΟΣ
ἀγάλλῃ;

ΑΓΑΥΗ
            γέγηθα,
μεγάλα μεγάλα καὶ
φανερὰ τᾷδ᾽ ἄγρᾳ κατειργασμένα.

ΧΟΡΟΣ
δεῖξόν νυν, ὦ τάλαινα, σὴν νικηφόρον   1200
ἀστοῖσιν ἄγραν ἣν φέρουσ᾽ ἐλήλυθας.

ΑΓΑΥΗ
ὦ καλλίπυργον ἄστυ Θηβαίας χθονὸς
ναίοντες, ἔλθεθ᾽ ὡς ἴδητε τήνδ᾽ ἄγραν,
Κάδμου θυγατέρες θηρὸς ἣν ἠγρεύσαμεν,
οὐκ ἀγκυλητοῖς Θεσσαλῶν στοχάσμασιν,   1205
οὐ δικτύοισιν, ἀλλὰ λευκοπήχεσι
χειρῶν ἀκμαῖσιν. κᾆτα κομπάζειν χρεὼν
καὶ λογχοποιῶν ὄργανα κτᾶσθαι μάτην;
ἡμεῖς δέ γ᾽ αὐτῇ χειρὶ τόνδε θ᾽ εἵλομεν,
χωρίς τε θηρὸς ἄρθρα διεφορήσαμεν.   1210
ποῦ μοι πατὴρ ὁ πρέσβυς; ἐλθέτω πέλας.
Πενθεύς τ᾽ ἐμὸς παῖς ποῦ ᾽στιν; αἱρέσθω λαβὼν
πηκτῶν πρὸς οἴκους κλιμάκων προσαμβάσεις,
ὡς πασσαλεύσῃ κρᾶτα τριγλύφοις τόδε
λέοντος ὃν πάρειμι θηράσασ᾽ ἐγώ.   1215

CHORUS

          . . . and Pentheus, your son, as well.

AGAVE

   . . . will celebrate his mother, who caught the beast,
just like a lion.

CHORUS

          It's a strange trophy.

AGAVE

   And strangely captured, too.

CHORUS

          You're proud of what you've done?

AGAVE

   Yes, I'm delighted. Great things I've done—
great things on this hunt, clear for all to see.

CHORUS

   Well then, you most unfortunate woman,   [1200]
show off your hunting prize, your sign of victory,
to all the citizens.

AGAVE [*addressing everyone*]

          All of you here,
all you living in the land of Thebes,
in this city with its splendid walls,
come see this wild beast we hunted down—
daughters of Cadmus—not with thonged spears,
Thessalian javelins, or by using nets,
but with our own white hands, our finger tips.
After this, why should huntsmen boast aloud,
when no one needs the implements they use?
We caught this beast by hand, tore it apart—   [1210]
with our own hands. But where's my father?
He should come here. And where's Pentheus?
Where is my son? He should take a ladder,
set it against the house, fix this lion's head
way up there, high on the palace front.
I've captured it and brought it home with me.

ΚΑΔΜΟΣ

ἕπεσθέ μοι φέροντες ἄθλιον βάρος
Πενθέως, ἕπεσθε, πρόσπολοι, δόμων πάρος,
οὗ σῶμα μοχθῶν μυρίοις ζητήμασιν
φέρω τόδ᾽, εὑρὼν ἐν Κιθαιρῶνος πτυχαῖς
διασπαρακτόν, κοὐδὲν ἐν ταὐτῷ πέδῳ   1220
λαβών, ἐν ὕλῃ κείμενον δυσευρέτῳ.
ἤκουσα γάρ του θυγατέρων τολμήματα,
ἤδη κατ᾽ ἄστυ τειχέων ἔσω βεβὼς
σὺν τῷ γέροντι Τειρεσίᾳ Βακχῶν πάρα·
πάλιν δὲ κάμψας εἰς ὄρος κομίζομαι   1225
τὸν κατθανόντα παῖδα Μαινάδων ὕπο.
καὶ τὴν μὲν Ἀκτέων᾽ Ἀρισταίῳ ποτὲ
τεκοῦσαν εἶδον Αὐτονόην Ἰνώ θ᾽ ἅμα
ἔτ᾽ ἀμφὶ δρυμοὺς οἰστροπλῆγας ἀθλίας,
τὴν δ᾽ εἶπέ τίς μοι δεῦρο βακχείῳ ποδὶ   1230
στείχειν Ἀγαύην, οὐδ᾽ ἄκραντ᾽ ἠκούσαμεν·
λεύσσω γὰρ αὐτήν, ὄψιν οὐκ εὐδαίμονα.

ἈΓΑΥΗ

πάτερ, μέγιστον κομπάσαι πάρεστί σοι,
πάντων ἀρίστας θυγατέρας σπεῖραι μακρῷ
θνητῶν· ἁπάσας εἶπον, ἐξόχως δ᾽ ἐμέ,   1235
ἣ τὰς παρ᾽ ἱστοῖς ἐκλιποῦσα κερκίδας
ἐς μεῖζον᾽ ἥκω, θῆρας ἀγρεύειν χεροῖν.
φέρω δ᾽ ἐν ὠλέναισιν, ὡς ὁρᾷς, τάδε
λαβοῦσα τἀριστεῖα, σοῖσι πρὸς δόμοις
ὡς ἀγκρεμασθῇ· σὺ δέ, πάτερ, δέξαι χεροῖν·   1240

[Enter Cadmus and attendants, carrying parts of Pentheus' body]

CADMUS

    Follow me, all those of you who carry
    some part of wretched Pentheus. You slaves,
    come here, right by the house.

[They place the bits of Pentheus' body together in a chest front of the palace]

                          I'm worn out.
  So many searches—but I picked up the body.
  I came across it in the rocky clefts
  on Mount Cithaeron, ripped to pieces,   [1220]
  no parts lying together in one place.
  It was in the woods—difficult to search.
  Someone told me what my daughter'd done,
  those horrific acts, once I'd come back,
  returning here with old Tiresias,
  inside the city walls, back from the Bacchae.
  So I climbed the mountains once again.
  Now I bring home this child the Maenads killed.
  I saw Autonoe, who once bore
  Actaeon to Aristeius—and Ino,
  she was with her there, in the forest,
  both still possessed, quite mad, poor creatures.
  Someone said Agave was coming here,   [1230]
  still doing her Bacchic dance. He spoke the truth,
  for I see her there—what a wretched sight!

AGAVE

    Father, now you can be truly proud.
    Among all living men you've produced
    by far the finest daughters. I'm talking
    of all of us, but especially of myself.
    I've left behind my shuttle and my loom,
    and risen to great things, catching wild beasts
    with my bare hands. Now I've captured him,
    I'm holding in my arms the finest trophy,
    as you can see, bringing it back home to you,
    so it may hang here.

    [offering him Pentheus' head]

                  Take this, father   [1240]
  let your hands welcome it. Be proud of it,

γαυρούμενος δὲ τοῖς ἐμοῖς ἀγρεύμασιν
κάλει φίλους ἐς δαῖτα· μακάριος γὰρ εἶ,
μακάριος, ἡμῶν τοιάδ᾽ ἐξειργασμένων.

ΚΑΔΜΟΣ

ὦ πένθος οὐ μετρητὸν οὐδ᾽ οἷόν τ᾽ ἰδεῖν,
φόνον ταλαίναις χερσὶν ἐξειργασμένων.   1245
καλὸν τὸ θῦμα καταβαλοῦσα δαίμοσιν
ἐπὶ δαῖτα Θήβας τάσδε κἀμὲ παρακαλεῖς.
οἴμοι κακῶν μὲν πρῶτα σῶν, ἔπειτ᾽ ἐμῶν·
ὡς ὁ θεὸς ἡμᾶς ἐνδίκως μέν, ἀλλ᾽ ἄγαν,
Βρόμιος ἄναξ ἀπώλεσ᾽ οἰκεῖος γεγώς.   1250

ΑΓΑΥΗ

ὡς δύσκολον τὸ γῆρας ἀνθρώποις ἔφυ
ἔν τ᾽ ὄμμασι σκυθρωπόν. εἴθε παῖς ἐμὸς
εὔθηρος εἴη, μητρὸς εἰκασθεὶς τρόποις,
ὅτ᾽ ἐν νεανίαισι Θηβαίοις ἅμα
θηρῶν ὀριγνῷτ᾽· ἀλλὰ θεομαχεῖν μόνον   1255
οἷός τ᾽ ἐκεῖνος. νουθετητέος, πάτερ,
σούστίν. τίς αὐτὸν δεῦρ᾽ ἂν ὄψιν εἰς ἐμὴν
καλέσειεν, ὡς ἴδῃ με τὴν εὐδαίμονα;

ΚΑΔΜΟΣ

φεῦ φεῦ· φρονήσασαι μὲν οἶ᾽ ἐδράσατε
ἀλγήσετ᾽ ἄλγος δεινόν· εἰ δὲ διὰ τέλους   1260
ἐν τῷδ᾽ ἀεὶ μενεῖτ᾽ ἐν ᾧ καθέστατε,
οὐκ εὐτυχοῦσαι δόξετ᾽ οὐχὶ δυστυχεῖν.

ΑΓΑΥΗ

τί δ᾽ οὐ καλῶς τῶνδ᾽ ἢ τί λυπηρῶς ἔχει;

ΚΑΔΜΟΣ

πρῶτον μὲν ἐς τόνδ᾽ αἰθέρ᾽ ὄμμα σὸν μέθες.

ΑΓΑΥΗ

ἰδού· τί μοι τόνδ᾽ ἐξυπεῖπας εἰσορᾶν;   1265

of what I've caught. Summon all your friends—
have a banquet, for you are blessed indeed,
blessed your daughters have achieved these things.

CADMUS

This grief's beyond measure, beyond endurance.
With these hands of yours you've murdered him.
You strike down this sacrificial victim,
this offering to the gods, then invite me,
and all of Thebes, to share a banquet.
Alas—first for your sorrow, then my own.
Lord god Bromius, born into this family,
has destroyed us, acting out his justice,   [1250]
but too much so.

AGAVE

                              Why such scowling eyes?
How sorrowful and solemn old men become.
As for my son, I hope he's a fine hunter,
who copies his mother's hunting style,
when he rides out with young men of Thebes
chasing after creatures in the wild.
The only thing he seems capable of doing
is fighting with the gods. It's up to you,
father, to reprimand him for it.
Who'll call him here into my sight,
so he can see my good luck for himself?

CADMUS

Alas! Alas! What dreadful pain you'll feel
when you recognize what you've just done.   [1260]
If you stay forever in your present state,
you'll be unfortunate, but you won't feel
as if you're suffering unhappiness.

AGAVE

But what in all this is wrong or painful?

CADMUS

First, raise your eyes. Look up into the sky.

AGAVE

All right. But why tell me to look up there?

ΚΑΔΜΟΣ

    ἔθ' αὑτὸς ἢ σοι μεταβολὰς ἔχειν δοκεῖ;

ἈΓΑΥΗ

    λαμπρότερος ἢ πρὶν καὶ διειπετέστερος.

ΚΑΔΜΟΣ

    τὸ δὲ πτοηθὲν τόδ' ἔτι σῇ ψυχῇ πάρα;

ἈΓΑΥΗ

    οὐκ οἶδα τοὔπος τοῦτο. γίγνομαι δέ πως
    ἔννους, μετασταθεῖσα τῶν πάρος φρενῶν.   1270

ΚΑΔΜΟΣ

    κλύοις ἂν οὖν τι κἀποκρίναι' ἂν σαφῶς;

ἈΓΑΥΗ

    ὡς ἐκλέλησμαί γ' ἃ πάρος εἴπομεν, πάτερ.

ΚΑΔΜΟΣ

    ἐς ποῖον ἦλθες οἶκον ὑμεναίων μέτα;

ἈΓΑΥΗ

    Σπαρτῷ μ' ἔδωκας, ὡς λέγουσ', Ἐχίονι.

ΚΑΔΜΟΣ

    τίς οὖν ἐν οἴκοις παῖς ἐγένετο σῷ πόσει;   1275

ἈΓΑΥΗ

    Πενθεύς, ἐμῇ τε καὶ πατρὸς κοινωνίᾳ.

ΚΑΔΜΟΣ

    τίνος πρόσωπον δῆτ' ἐν ἀγκάλαις ἔχεις;

ἈΓΑΥΗ

    λέοντος, ὥς γ' ἔφασκον αἱ θηρώμεναι.

CADMUS

> Does the sky still seem the same to you,
> or has it changed?

AGAVE

> It seems, well, brighter . . .
> more translucent than it was before.

CADMUS

> And your inner spirit — is it still shaking?

AGAVE

> I don't understand what it is you're asking.
> But my mind is starting to clear somehow.
> It's changing . . . it's not what it was before.   [1270]

CADMUS

> Can you hear me? Can you answer clearly?

AGAVE

> Yes. But, father, what we discussed before,
> I've quite forgotten.

CADMUS

> Then tell me this —
> to whose house did you come when you got married?

AGAVE

> You gave me to Echion, who, men say,
> was one of those who grew from seeds you cast.

CADMUS

> In that house you bore your husband a child.
> What was his name?

AGAVE

> His name was Pentheus.
> I conceived him with his father.

CADMUS

> Well then,
> this head your hands are holding — whose is it?

AGAVE

> It's a lion's. That's what the hunters said.

ΚΑΔΜΟΣ

σκέψαι νυν ὀρθῶς· βραχὺς ὁ μόχθος εἰσιδεῖν.

ἈΓΑΥΗ

ἔα, τί λεύσσω; τί φέρομαι τόδ᾽ ἐν χεροῖν;   1280

ΚΑΔΜΟΣ

ἄθρησον αὐτὸ καὶ σαφέστερον μάθε.

ἈΓΑΥΗ

ὁρῶ μέγιστον ἄλγος ἡ τάλαιν᾽ ἐγώ.

ΚΑΔΜΟΣ

μῶν σοι λέοντι φαίνεται προσεικέναι;

ἈΓΑΥΗ

οὔκ, ἀλλὰ Πενθέως ἡ τάλαιν᾽ ἔχω κάρα.

ΚΑΔΜΟΣ

ᾠμωγμένον γε πρόσθεν ἢ σὲ γνωρίσαι.   1285

ἈΓΑΥΗ

τίς ἔκτανέν νιν; —πῶς ἐμὰς ἦλθεν χέρας;

ΚΑΔΜΟΣ

δύστην᾽ ἀλήθει᾽, ὡς ἐν οὐ καιρῷ πάρει.

ἈΓΑΥΗ

λέγ᾽, ὡς τὸ μέλλον καρδία πήδημ᾽ ἔχει.

ΚΑΔΜΟΣ

σύ νιν κατέκτας καὶ κασίγνηται σέθεν.

ἈΓΑΥΗ

ποῦ δ᾽ ὤλετ᾽; ἦ κατ᾽ οἶκον; ἢ ποίοις τόποις;   1290

CADMUS

    Inspect it carefully. You can do that
    without much effort.

AGAVE *[inspecting the head]*

                          What is this?
    What am I looking at? What am I holding?   [1280]

CADMUS

    Look at it. You'll understand more clearly.

AGAVE

    What I see fills me with horrific pain . . .
    such agony . . .

CADMUS

                  Does it still seem to you
    to be a lion's head?

AGAVE

                  No. It's appalling—
    this head I'm holding belongs to Pentheus.

CADMUS

    Yes, that's right. I was lamenting his fate
    before you recognized him.

AGAVE

              Who killed him?
    How did he come into my hands?

CADMUS

                 Harsh truth—
    how you come to light at the wrong moment.

AGAVE

    Tell me. My heart is pounding in me
    to hear what you're about to say.

CADMUS

             You killed him—
    you and your sisters.

AGAVE

          Where was he killed?
    At home? In what sort of place?   [1290]

ΚΑΔΜΟΣ
 οὗπερ πρὶν Ἀκτέωνα διέλαχον κύνες.

ΆΓΑΥΗ
 τί δ᾽ ἐς Κιθαιρῶν᾽ ἦλθε δυσδαίμων ὅδε;

ΚΑΔΜΟΣ
 ἐκερτόμει θεὸν σάς τε βακχείας μολών.

ΆΓΑΥΗ
 ἡμεῖς δ᾽ ἐκεῖσε τίνι τρόπῳ κατήραμεν;

ΚΑΔΜΟΣ
 ἐμάνητε, πᾶσά τ᾽ ἐξεβακχεύθη πόλις.   1295

ΆΓΑΥΗ
 Διόνυσος ἡμᾶς ὤλεσ᾽, ἄρτι μανθάνω.

ΚΑΔΜΟΣ
 ὕβριν γ᾽ ὑβρισθείς· θεὸν γὰρ οὐχ ἡγεῖσθέ νιν.

ΆΓΑΥΗ
 τὸ φίλτατον δὲ σῶμα ποῦ παιδός, πάτερ;

ΚΑΔΜΟΣ
 ἐγὼ μόλις τόδ᾽ ἐξερευνήσας φέρω.

ΆΓΑΥΗ
 ἦ πᾶν ἐν ἄρθροις συγκεκλημένον καλῶς;   1300

ΚΑΔΜΟΣ
 <...>

ΆΓΑΥΗ
 Πενθεῖ δὲ τί μέρος ἀφροσύνης προσῆκ᾽ ἐμῆς;

ΚΑΔΜΟΣ
 ὑμῖν ἐγένεθ᾽ ὅμοιος, οὐ σέβων θεόν.
 τοιγὰρ συνῆψε πάντας ἐς μίαν βλάβην,
 ὑμᾶς τε τόνδε θ᾽, ὥστε διολέσαι δόμους
 κἄμ᾽, ὅστις ἄτεκνος ἀρσένων παίδων γεγὼς   1305

CADMUS

                                    He was killed
where dogs once made a common meal of Actaeon.

AGAVE

Why did this poor man go to Cithaeron?

CADMUS

He went there to ridicule the god
and you for celebrating Dionysus.

AGAVE

But how did we happen to be up there?

CADMUS

You were insane—the entire city
was in a Bacchic madness.

AGAVE

                         Now I see.
Dionysus has destroyed us all.

CADMUS

He took offense at being insulted.
You did not consider him a god.

AGAVE

Father, where's the body of my dearest son?

CADMUS

I had trouble tracking the body down.
I brought back what I found.

AGAVE

                  Are all his limbs laid out
just as they should be? And Pentheus,   [1300]
what part did he play in my madness?

CADMUS

Like you, he was irreverent to the god.
That's why the god linked you and him together
in the same disaster—thus destroying
the house and me, for I've no children left,

113

τῆς σῆς τόδ' ἔρνος, ὦ τάλαινα, νηδύος
αἴσχιστα καὶ κάκιστα κατθανόνθ' ὁρῶ,
ᾧ δῶμ' ἀνέβλεφ'—ὃς συνεῖχες, ὦ τέκνον,
τοὐμὸν μέλαθρον, παιδὸς ἐξ ἐμῆς γεγώς,
πόλει τε τάρβος ἦσθα· τὸν γέροντα δὲ   1310
οὐδεὶς ὑβρίζειν ἤθελ' εἰσορῶν τὸ σὸν
κάρα· δίκην γὰρ ἀξίαν ἐλάμβανες.
νῦν δ' ἐκ δόμων ἄτιμος ἐκβεβλήσομαι
ὁ Κάδμος ὁ μέγας, ὃς τὸ Θηβαίων γένος
ἔσπειρα κἀξήμησα κάλλιστον θέρος.   1315
ὦ φίλτατ' ἀνδρῶν—καὶ γὰρ οὐκέτ' ὢν ὅμως
τῶν φιλτάτων ἔμοιγ' ἀριθμήσῃ, τέκνον—
οὐκέτι γενείου τοῦδε θιγγάνων χερί,
τὸν μητρὸς αὐδῶν πατέρα προσπτύξῃ, τέκνον,
λέγων· Τίς ἀδικεῖ, τίς σ' ἀτιμάζει, γέρον;   1320
τίς σὴν ταράσσει καρδίαν λυπηρὸς ὤν;
λέγ', ὡς κολάζω τὸν ἀδικοῦντά σ', ὦ πάτερ.
νῦν δ' ἄθλιος μέν εἰμ' ἐγώ, τλήμων δὲ σύ.
οἰκτρὰ δὲ μήτηρ, τλήμονες δὲ σύγγονοι.
εἰ δ' ἔστιν ὅστις δαιμόνων ὑπερφρονεῖ,   1325
ἐς τοῦδ' ἀθρήσας θάνατον ἡγείσθω θεούς.

ΧΟΡΟΣ
    τὸ μὲν σὸν ἀλγῶ, Κάδμε· σὸς δ' ἔχει δίκην
    παῖς παιδὸς ἀξίαν μέν, ἀλγεινὴν δὲ σοί.

ἈΓΑΥΗ
    ὦ πάτερ, ὁρᾷς γὰρ τἄμ' ὅσῳ μετεστράφη

. . .

now I see this offspring of your womb,
you unhappy woman, cruelly butchered
in the most shameful way. He was the one
who brought new vision to our family.

[addressing the remains of Pentheus]

My child, you upheld the honour of our house,
my daughter's son. You were feared in Thebes.   [1310]
No one who saw you ever would insult me,
though I was old, for you would then inflict
fit punishment. Now the mighty Cadmus,
the man who sowed and later harvested
the most splendid crop — the Theban people —
will be an exile, banished from his home,
a dishonoured man. Dearest of men,
even though, my child, you're alive no more,
I count you among those closest to me.
You won't be touching my cheek any more,
holding me in your arms, and calling me
"grandfather," as you ask me, "Old man,
who's injuring or dishonouring you?   [1320]
Who upsets your heart with any pain?
Tell me, father, so I can punish him —
anyone who treats you in an unjust way."
Now you're in this horrifying state,
I'm in misery, your mother's pitiful,
and all your relatives are in despair.
If there's a man who disrespects the gods,
let him think about how this man perished —
then he should develop faith in them.

CHORUS LEADER

I'm sorry for you Cadmus — you're in pain.
But your grandson deserved his punishment.

AGAVE

Father, you see how all has changed for me.[12]
[From being your royal and honoured daughter,
the mother of a king, I'm now transformed —
an abomination, something to fill
all people's hearts with horror, with disgust —
the mother who slaughtered her only son,

. . .

. . .

. . .

who tore him apart, ripping out the heart
from the child who filled her own heart with joy—
all to honour this god Dionysus.
But, father, give me your permission now
to lay out here the body of my son,
prepare his corpse for proper burial.

CADMUS

That's no easy task to undertake.
His body, all the parts I could collect,
lies here, in this chest, not a pretty sight.
My own eyes can hardly bear to see him.
But if you think you can endure the work,
then, my child, begin the appropriate rites.

AGAVE *[removing Pentheus' limbs and placing them on the ground in front of her]*
Alas, for my poor son, my only child,
destroyed by his mother's Bacchic madness.
How could these hands of mine, which loved him so,
have torn these limbs apart, ripped out his flesh.
Here's an arm which has held me all these years,
growing stronger as he grew into a man,
his feet . . . O how he used to run to me,
seeking assurance of his mother's love.
His face was handsome, on the verge of manhood.
See the soft down still resting on these lips,
which have kissed me thousands of times or more.
All this, and all the rest, set here before us.
Oh Zeus and all you Olympian gods . . . .

[She cannot complete the ritual and collapses in grief]

It makes no sense—it's unendurable.
How could the god have wished such things on me?

CHORUS LEADER *[helping Agave get up]*
Lady, you must bear what cannot be borne.
Your suffering is intense, but the god is just.
You insulted him in Thebes, showed no respect—
you've brought the punishment upon yourself.

CHORUS

What is wisdom? What is finer
than the rights men get from gods—

. . .

. . .

ΔΙΟΝΥΣΟΣ

δράκων γενήσῃ μεταβαλών, δάμαρ τε σὴ   1330
ἐκθηριωθεῖσ᾽ ὄφεος ἀλλάξει τύπον,
ἣν Ἄρεος ἔσχες Ἁρμονίαν θνητὸς γεγώς.
ὄχον δὲ μόσχων, χρησμὸς ὡς λέγει Διός,
ἐλᾷς μετ᾽ ἀλόχου, βαρβάρων ἡγούμενος.
πολλὰς δὲ πέρσεις ἀναρίθμῳ στρατεύματι   1335
πόλεις· ὅταν δὲ Λοξίου χρηστήριον
διαρπάσωσι, νόστον ἄθλιον πάλιν
σχήσουσι· σὲ δ᾽ Ἄρης Ἁρμονίαν τε ῥύσεται
μακάρων τ᾽ ἐς αἶαν σὸν καθιδρύσει βίον.
ταῦτ᾽ οὐχὶ θνητοῦ πατρὸς ἐκγεγὼς λέγω   1340
Διόνυσος, ἀλλὰ Ζηνός· εἰ δὲ σωφρονεῖν
ἔγνωθ᾽, ὅτ᾽ οὐκ ἠθέλετε, τὸν Διὸς γόνον
εὐδαιμονεῖτ᾽ ἂν σύμμαχον κεκτημένοι.

to hold their powerful hands
over the heads of their enemies?
Ah yes, what's good is always loved.
So all praise Dionysus,
praise the dancing god,
god of our revelry,
god whose justice is divine,
whose justice now reveals itself.

[Enter Dionysus]

DIONYSUS

Yes, I am Dionysus, son of Zeus.
You see me now before you as a god.
You Thebans learned about my powers too late.
Dishonouring me, you earn the penalty.
You refused my rites. Now you must leave —
abandon your city for barbarian lands.
Agave, too, that polluted creature,
must go into perpetual banishment.
And Cadmus, you too must endure your lot.][13]
Your form will change, so you become a dragon.   [1330]
Your wife, Harmonia, Ares' daughter,
whom you, though mortal, took in marriage,
will be transformed, changing to a snake.
As Zeus' oracle declares, you and she
will drive a chariot drawn by heifers.
You'll rule barbarians. With your armies,
too large to count, you'll raze many cities.
Once they despoil Apollo's oracle,
they'll have a painful journey back again.
But Ares will guard you and Harmonia.
In lands of the blessed he'll transform your lives.
That's what I proclaim — I, Dionysus,   [1340]
born from no mortal father, but from Zeus.
If you had understood how to behave
as you should have when you were unwilling,
you'd now be fortunate, with Zeus' child
among your allies.

ΚΑΔΜΟΣ
Διόνυσε, λισσόμεσθά σ᾽, ἠδικήκαμεν.

ΔΙΟΝΥΣΟΣ
ὄψ᾽ ἐμάθεθ᾽ ἡμᾶς, ὅτε δὲ χρῆν, οὐκ ᾔδετε.   1345

ΚΑΔΜΟΣ
ἐγνώκαμεν ταῦτ᾽· ἀλλ᾽ ἐπεξέρχῃ λίαν.

ΔΙΟΝΥΣΟΣ
καὶ γὰρ πρὸς ὑμῶν θεὸς γεγὼς ὑβριζόμην.

ΚΑΔΜΟΣ
ὀργὰς πρέπει θεοὺς οὐχ ὁμοιοῦσθαι βροτοῖς.

ΔΙΟΝΥΣΟΣ
πάλαι τάδε Ζεὺς οὑμὸς ἐπένευσεν πατήρ.

ἈΓΑΥΗ
αἰαῖ, δέδοκται, πρέσβυ, τλήμονες φυγαί.   1350

ΔΙΟΝΥΣΟΣ
τί δῆτα μέλλεθ᾽ ἅπερ ἀναγκαίως ἔχει;

ΚΑΔΜΟΣ
ὦ τέκνον, ὡς ἐς δεινὸν ἤλθομεν κακὸν
πάντες, σύ θ᾽ ἡ τάλαινα σύγγονοί τε σαί,
ἐγώ θ᾽ ὁ τλήμων· βαρβάρους ἀφίξομαι
γέρων μέτοικος· ἔτι δέ μοι τὸ θέσφατον   1355
ἐς Ἑλλάδ᾽ ἀγαγεῖν μιγάδα βάρβαρον στρατόν.
καὶ τὴν Ἄρεως παῖδ᾽ Ἁρμονίαν, δάμαρτ᾽ ἐμήν,
δράκων δρακαίνης φύσιν ἔχουσαν ἀγρίαν
ἄξω 'πὶ βωμοὺς καὶ τάφους Ἑλληνικούς,
ἡγούμενος λόγχαισιν· οὐδὲ παύσομαι   1360
κακῶν ὁ τλήμων, οὐδὲ τὸν καταιβάτην
Ἀχέροντα πλεύσας ἥσυχος γενήσομαι.

CADMUS

                            O Dionysus,
we implore you—we've not acted justly.

DIONYSUS

You learn too late. You were ignorant
when you should have known.

CADMUS

                         Now we understand.
Your actions against us are too severe.

DIONYSUS

I was born a god, and you insulted me.

CADMUS

Angry gods should not act just like humans.

DIONYSUS

My father Zeus willed all this long ago.

AGAVE

Alas, old man, then this must be our fate,   [1350]
a miserable exile.

DIONYSUS

                     Why then delay?
Why postpone what necessity requires?

CADMUS

Child, we've stumbled into this disaster,
this terrible calamity—you and me,
both in agony—your sisters, too.
So I'll go out to the barbarians,
a foreign resident in my old age.
And then for me there's that oracle
which says I'll lead a mixed barbarian force
back into Greece. And I'll bring here with me
Harmonia, Ares' daughter, my wife.
I'll have the savage nature of a snake,
as I lead my soldiers to the altars,
to the tombs, in Greece. But even then,
there'll be no end to my wretched sorrows.   [1360]
I'll never sail the downward plunging Acheron
and reach some final peace.

121

ἈΓΑΥΗ
ὦ πάτερ, ἐγὼ δὲ σοῦ στερεῖσα φεύξομαι.

ΚΑΔΜΟΣ
τί μ᾽ ἀμφιβάλλεις χερσίν, ὦ τάλαινα παῖ,
ὄρνις ὅπως κηφῆνα πολιόχρων κύκνος;   1365

ἈΓΑΥΗ
ποῖ γὰρ τράπωμαι πατρίδος ἐκβεβλημένη;

ΚΑΔΜΟΣ
οὐκ οἶδα, τέκνον· μικρὸς ἐπίκουρος πατήρ.

ἈΓΑΥΗ
χαῖρ᾽, ὦ μέλαθρον, χαῖρ᾽, ὦ πατρία
πόλις· ἐκλείπω σ᾽ ἐπὶ δυστυχίᾳ
φυγὰς ἐκ θαλάμων.   1370

ΚΑΔΜΟΣ
στεῖχέ νυν, ὦ παῖ, τὸν Ἀρισταίου ...

ἈΓΑΥΗ
στένομαί σε, πάτερ.

ΚΑΔΜΟΣ
                    κἀγὼ σέ, τέκνον,
καὶ σὰς ἐδάκρυσα κασιγνήτας.

ἈΓΑΥΗ
δεινῶς γὰρ τάνδ᾽ αἰκείαν
Διόνυσος ἄναξ τοὺς σοὺς εἰς   1375
οἴκους ἔφερεν.

ΔΙΟΝΥΣΟΣ
καὶ γὰρ ἔπασχον δεινὰ πρὸς ὑμῶν,
ἀγέραστον ἔχων ὄνομ᾽ ἐν Θήβαις.

ἈΓΑΥΗ
χαῖρε, πάτερ, μοι.

AGAVE *[embracing Cadmus]*
> Father, I must be exiled without you.

CADMUS
> Why do you throw your arms about me,
> my unhappy child, just like some young swan
> protecting an old one—gray and helpless.

AGAVE
> Because I've no idea where to go,
> once I'm banished from my father's land.

CADMUS
> Child, I don't know. Your father's not much help.

AGAVE
> Farewell, then, to my home.
> Farewell to my native city.
> In my misfortune I abandon you,
> an exile from spaces once my own.   [1370]

CADMUS
> Go now to Aristeus' house, my child.14

AGAVE
> How I grieve for you, my father.

CADMUS
> And I grieve for you, my child,
> as I weep for your sisters.

AGAVE
> Lord Dionysus has inflicted
> such brutal terror on your house.

DIONYSUS:
> Yes. For at your hands I suffered, too—
> and dreadfully. For here in Thebes
> my name received no recognition.

AGAVE
> Farewell, father.

Euripides

ΚΑΔΜΟΣ

χαῖρ᾽, ὦ μελέα
θύγατερ. χαλεπῶς δ᾽ ἐς τόδ᾽ ἂν ἥκοις.　　　　　1380

ΑΓΑΥΗ

ἄγετ᾽, ὦ πομποί, με κασιγνήτας
ἵνα συμφυγάδας ληψόμεθ᾽ οἰκτράς.
ἔλθοιμι δ᾽ ὅπου
μήτε Κιθαιρὼν ἔμ᾽ ἴδοι μιαρὸς
μήτε Κιθαιρῶν᾽ ὄσσοισιν ἐγώ,　　　　　1385
μήθ᾽ ὅθι θύρσου μνῆμ᾽ ἀνάκειται·
Βάκχαις δ᾽ ἄλλαισι μέλοιεν.

ΧΟΡΟΣ

πολλαὶ μορφαὶ τῶν δαιμονίων,
πολλὰ δ᾽ ἀέλπτως κραίνουσι θεοί·
καὶ τὰ δοκηθέντ᾽ οὐκ ἐτελέσθη,　　　　　1390
τῶν δ᾽ ἀδοκήτων πόρον ηὖρε θεός.
τοιόνδ᾽ ἀπέβη τόδε πρᾶγμα.

CADMUS

> My most unhappy daughter,
> may you fare well. That will be hard for you.   [1380]

AGAVE

> Lead on, friends, so I may take my sisters,
> those pitiful women, into exile with me.
> May I go somewhere where cursed Cithaeron
> will never see me, nor my eyes glimpse
> that dreadful mountain, a place far away
> from any sacred thyrsus. Let others
> make Bacchic celebrations their concern.

[Exit Agave]

CHORUS

> The gods appear in many forms,
> carrying with them unwelcome things.
> What people thought would happen never did.
> What they did not expect, the gods made happen.
> That's what this story has revealed.

[Exeunt Chorus and Cadmus, leaving on stage the remains of Pentheus' body]

NOTES

1. Semele, Cadmus' daughter and Dionysus' mother, had an affair with Zeus. Hera, Zeus' wife, tricked Zeus into destroying Semele with a lightning bolt. Zeus took the infant Dionysus from his mother's womb as she was dying and sewed him into his thigh, where Dionysus continued to grow until he was delivered as a new-born infant.

2. A *thyrsus* (pl. *thyrsoi*) is a hollow plant stalk, usually decorated with ivy, and carried as a symbol of Dionysus in the dancing celebrations (where it can acquire magical powers).

3. The Maenads, who make up the Chorus of the play, are the female followers of Dionysus, who have followed him from Phrygia in Asia Minor to Thebes.

4. Rhea is Zeus' mother. The drums are tambourines. Tmolus is a mountain in Asia Minor. Mount Cithaeron is a sacred mountain near Thebes.

5. Bromius and Bacchus are alternate names for Dionysus.

6. Cybele is an eastern mother goddess. The Curetes and Corybantes are attendants on the goddess Cybele. They banged their drums to drown out the cries of the infant Zeus, whose mother, Rhea, was trying to protect him from his father, Cronos.

7. Evoë is a cry of celebration in the Dionysian rituals.

8. Sidon, in Asia Minor, as these lines inform was, was the place where the royal family of Thebes originated. Cadmus had come from Asia Minor, sent out from home by his father, and founded Thebes.

9. Agave (Pentheus' mother), Ino, and Autonoe were sisters, all daughters of Cadmus. Actaeon, son of Autonoe, offended the goddess Artemis, who turned him into a stag and had him torn apart by his own hunting dogs (see line 429 below).

10. The term *barbarian* refers to non-Greek-speaking people.

11. Pentheus' father Echion was one of the warriors born when Cadmus, on instructions from the gods, killed a serpent-dragon and sowed its teeth in the earth. The teeth germinated as warriors rising from the ground.

12. At this point, there is a major gap in the manuscript. The text here is reconstructed from what we know about the content of the missing portion.

13. The Greek text resumes here at the end of the gap in the manuscript.

14. Aristeus is the husband of Autonoe and father of Actaeon.